Light OF Victory

THE TRUE STORY OF MY TOTAL
DELIVERANCE FROM FEAR, ANXIETY, AND DEPRESSION

DR. CHARLES GREEN

Light of Victory: The True Story of My Total Deliverance from Fear, Anxiety and Depression, by Dr. Charles Green

copyright ©2020 Charles Green

ISBN: 978-1-950718-44-3

published by Kudu Publishing

cover design by Martijn van Tilborgh

Light of Victory is available in Amazon Kindle, Barnes & Noble Nook and Apple iBooks.

*Dedicated to the memory of my dear wife,
Barbara Green, who became the light of my life,
and with lovingkindness, empathy, and great faith,
walked with me successfully through the journey
and went to be with Jesus on September 10, 2018.*

Contents

Foreword

BIG THINGS OFTEN START small. And sometimes, life-long relationships develop from five-minute hallway meetings.

As a seventeen-year-old high school junior, I had one such meeting, and it started one such relationship. That's when I met Dr. Charles Green at Word of Faith Temple, the New Orleans church he and his wife, Barbara, founded and pastored for more than fifty years. Their son Michael (who also became a pastor) and I both sang in our high school's select choir, and the two of us had stopped by the church while running errands.

I don't remember our exact conversation. What I do remember is that Dr. Green (known to me as "Pastor Charles") shared words of life. With the authority of a prophet, he spoke truth over me before I believed it myself. In what I now recognize as a Spirit-led appointment, he called me to come up higher.

I did just that two years later, when I committed myself to Christ. He became my Savior and Lord. Thanks in part to Pastor Charles' encouragement and example, I've been climbing ever since.

The second time I met this man of God was at the memorial service for Oral Roberts. At the time, I was serving as the dean of the College of Business at Oral Roberts University (ORU). I don't know why I recognized him, but I remember telling my wife, "There's Charles Green!"

I jumped up to meet him as if he were a home-run hitter for the St. Louis Cardinals. I'm pretty sure he thought I was a nut! I didn't know then that he had served on Chancellor Roberts' board of regents and was chairman of the Executive Board. In fact, throughout most of Roberts' ministry, Pastor Charles was his close friend and advisor.

Was it a simple coincidence that God sent me to ORU thirty-five years after my first conversation with Pastor Charles? It seems to me He had ORU in mind when He arranged for us to meet way back in 1971.

After coming to work at Charisma Media, I learned that our founder and CEO, Stephen Strang, has known Pastor Charles and Michael for many years. Another coincidence? I think not.

I believe I work, serve, and lead today because Pastor Charles planted an effectual seed in my life. Leaders often do what they do without many opportunities to learn of the impact of their work. I ministered the gospel for more than thirty years without Pastor Charles' knowledge, and I know his influence on me has changed the young people I've met along the way.

The impact of one short meeting can reach generations. The impact of one book can do the same. I'm grateful Pastor Charles has recorded his incredible story and wisdom within these pages, so he can touch many more hearts with his words of life.

Thank you, Pastor Charles. And thank you, God, for the inspired legacy of a man who follows You so faithfully.

—Dr. Steve Greene
Lake Mary, Florida

Acknowledgments

THERE ARE MANY PEOPLE to whom I am grateful. This book would not have been written if I had not lived the life I have described or had relationships with the great people who have been part of my life.

I want to thank my children, Michael Green and Cynthia Green Crider, for their love and devotion to Barbara and me. I thank God for their loving us, but even more for their love for the Lord Jesus Christ and for the lives they have lived, dedicated to the ministry.

I thank Dr. Steve Greene for his advice, counsel, and encouragement in writing this book. I have known Steve since he was seventeen years old. You will read more about this in his Foreword to the book.

I thank my dear friend Kenneth Copeland, whom I have known for over fifty-two years. What he has done to bless and encourage me could not be told on one page—it would take another book. His children and pastors of Eagle Mountain International Church, George and Terri Pearsons, have treated me like a dear father and blessed me in so many ways, helping to support my ministry while I was writing this book.

Thanks to Dr. Ernest Weaver who helped me in the beginning of this book. I greatly appreciate his advice and encouragement. He calls me his pastor.

I am indebted to the people who wrote such wonderful words about my book—Kenneth Copeland, Dr. Glenda Payas, and my sons in the Lord, Bishop Bart Pierce and Bishop Gordon McDonald.

Finally, I want to thank my four pastors, who loved me, tolerated me, and helped to train me for my ministry, making it possible for me to reach out to the world with the powerful riches of the gospel of the Kingdom of God. These were D. Frank Warren, William H. "Bill" Marshall, Marvin Hansford, and William A. McCann. They are all in heaven now, but their influence will live on long after I have joined them.

—*Charles Green*
Frisco, Texas

Introduction

WHEN PEOPLE CAME TO me as their pastor or as a friend and wanted to talk to me about depression, anxiety, or fear, it would usually go something like this:

"Pastor, I can't sleep at nights. I'm filled with fear. What am I going to do?"

"Don't worry about it. Forget it, and just act as if it were not there. It will soon go away."

"I've tried that. It hasn't worked."

Then the tears would come, and I would say, "Come on, let's pray about it." I would pray a nice little prayer and send them on their way.

I had a problem, but I didn't know it. I never believed it could happen to me.

Then one day, when I was a grown man with a wife and two small children, the roof caved in. I woke up one morning feeling something strange pressing down on me. I couldn't feel it physically, but it was there, nonetheless.

I had a problem I didn't understand, but by the time it was over, I could define it and describe it in detail. Because of it, I learned how to trust God in a new and more complete way, and what is more important, I learned to use the Word of God like a weapon of warfare. I also learned more about my own life and the history of my relationship with God.

I have quoted a few songs and choruses in this book. You see, my dad was a music teacher, and music was a part of my life from an early age.

During all my struggles, I did not leave the ministry. I did not blame God. My marriage and my family remained intact. When my deliverance came, I had learned how to walk out of darkness into the brilliant light of God's freedom.

In the chapters ahead, I will give you the story of my liberation from fear, anxiety, and depression. It came in one night, really in one moment. The method God used to bring deliverance to me is one that everyone can use. And it works! What really happened is that I went back to what I had learned but was not practicing.

I will also share with you the mystery of the little light bulb that went out and why it was so important to me. This is a great revelation that I have shared with people all over the world. I also want to share some important things about the ministry, the call of God upon our lives, and what it means "to hear from God."

This is personal. I am not going to direct this to "people" or "ministers" in a general way. This is for *you*. It is important to be able to hear from God. Those who want to be leaders in the Kingdom of God *must* be able to hear from God. It is so important that I make this definitive statement: "If you cannot hear from God, you cannot lead God's people." When God is speaking to us, it is important not only to listen but to obey.

Of course, I am going to tell you the central fact of my ultimate victory, but more than that, I shall deal with many struggles in my life and ministry. The vital thing for you to know is this: I have never lost a battle. Every enterprise I have ever started has been successful. I have never failed in any undertaking. In my life I have pastored three churches, and they have all greatly prospered, never experienced a church split. I never left any place where I could not go back and be accepted with open arms.

Some who read this book have problems like the ones that tormented me. Others have different concerns. Whatever the problem, whatever the battle, I will give you some secrets of survival and ultimate victory.

After you read of my miracle deliverance, please don't stop reading. I will show you in detail how you can live without crippling fear—what to believe and what to do so you can walk in health, freedom, and joy.

SECTION I: **SEASON OF DARKNESS**

CHAPTER 1

A Dark Journey

THE BEDROOM WAS DARK. I walked to the window and carefully pulled back the drapes just enough to see outside.

The light was out!

I had a difficult time breathing. Panic! My hand pushed on my chest. I pulled the drape back once again and looked frantically out into the street of total darkness. It was still extinguished. The light was still out.

It was only a small, naked light bulb, hanging from a pole across the street from our house. But night after night, when I could not sleep, when anxiety and torment filled my mind, I would leave the bed, walk to the window, pull back the drape and stare for an hour or more at the light. I did not understand it, but staring at that light brought me some comfort.

I had stood there, night after night, my eyes fixed on the little light, asking God to help me keep my sanity until the sun came up in the morning. It seemed things were better—not all right, but better—when daylight came.

During the day, I went about my routine like a mechanical man, a robot. I was weary, sleepy, and constantly disturbed. I lived with anxiety, fear, and torment. Each afternoon, as the daylight began to fade, I felt as if the darkness that was coming to the earth was also covering me. I could feel myself slipping into a deep, lonely hole.

Breathing didn't come naturally; I had to remember to do it. I would feel as if I were fainting and then realize I hadn't been breathing. My mind was a motor that would not stop. Thoughts—frightening thoughts—kept turning over and over in my brain.

I called the electric company at seven in the morning—at eight—and then at nine.

"Sir, the light is out!"

When a man finally answered, I tried not to sound frantic. But I was. I had walked the floor of the living room and kitchen through the night, being careful not to wake Barbara and the children: Michael, eight, and Cynthia, six.

"Sir, we really need that light put back in operation. Where we live is very dark (true) and dangerous (perhaps, but not likely), and we need that light working again as soon as possible!"

At the time, I did not know why the little light was so important to me. Today, I know the answer. I not only know why it was important; I also know why it comforted me. My terrible bout of fear, torment, anxiety, and depression started when I was thirty-five years old and lasted over seven months, into my thirty-sixth year.

Why was I so filled with fear? One night, I was standing at the back door of the first home we had built in the New Orleans area. I looked out at the vacant property next to our house, and I asked myself the question—the same question I had asked many times before. *What are you really afraid of? Or about?*

HOW IT BEGAN

I woke up one morning with a strange feeling. It was like a fog over my brain. There were lurking thoughts I could not define and questions I could not quickly answer.

What is this?

Have I forgotten something important I'm trying to remember?

Is it something I've done or said that I should not have done or said?

Oh, God, if that's what it is, let me know, and I will quickly tell You I'm sorry. I will repent and ask forgiveness.

Still, I did not think all this was important. I did not understand it, but it wasn't a big deal. It was only a crazy feeling for the moment. It was just a passing mood—or so I thought.

I remember saying to myself, *It will be gone in a little while. Whatever it is, I will work it out and have an answer soon, if not today, certainly when I wake up tomorrow.*

I sounded a lot like Scarlett O'Hara handled her problems in *Gone with the Wind*. "I won't think about that today. I'll think about it tomorrow."

It didn't work. I thought about it that day, every day, and on into the night, every night.

I tried to handle it the way I handled everybody else's fears, anxieties, and torments. "Pastor, I have a lot of fear in my life. I'm filled with anxiety. What am I going to do?"

I had a memorized answer: "Just snap out of it. Put it out of your mind. Tomorrow it will all be over."

So, I took my own advice. I told myself, *Get control of yourself. This is some foolish feeling. When you wake up tomorrow, it will all be gone.*

Little did I realize that on that day, I was sinking into a hellish emotional hole. I was beginning a journey of dark fear and torment that would last for many months. This journey would affect my mind, my marriage, my ministry—everything. Over and over, I would ask the same question: "Why?

"THIS CAN'T BE HAPPENING TO ME!"

These were the words I told myself over and over. But it *was* happening—to me! For a few weeks, no one knew. No one!

I did not tell my closest friends. I did not tell the elders of our church. I did not go to a doctor. And worst of all, I did not tell my wife, Barbara.

I didn't know what to tell her. I didn't know what to tell anybody. I didn't know what to tell myself. But I did talk to myself: *I'm not like this. Other people get nervous and struggle with fear, but not I. I'm a preacher. I'm a pastor. I'm supposed to have all the answers—even the word of faith. What will people say if I try to tell them what I'm experiencing—what I'm feeling?*

I knew what they would ask. "What secret sin have you committed? What have you been doing wrong?"

The answers were "none" and "nothing."

I tried to repent of things I had never done, and when I met people for the first time, I felt like apologizing, just in case I would say something or do something in the future that would hurt or harm them.

So, I just told myself, *I know what to do. I've told others what to do, and now I will do it. I'll just get so involved in my work, in my ministry, that I won't have time to worry, fret, or feel anxiety.*

This plan didn't work. Not only did I suffer at night, but I also had problems at work. Suddenly, I wanted no confrontations of any kind. No problems. I had no reason to fear; nevertheless, I felt as if every person coming toward me was going to attack me. So, I ran away.

I did not leave town, but I left the people. My office had been in a little room on the side of the platform in the church, but I decided to move to another location. I found a little closet on the second floor of the building. It only measured eight feet by ten feet, but I moved my office into that little closet, so no one could find me. But that was not enough. I began to park my car on the street behind the church. It was a block and a half away, but I didn't mind.

I was hiding. Hiding from problems, and therefore, hiding from people. I had learned the formula: When you have people, you have problems.

During this time, I would wait until the last minute every Sunday to walk into the auditorium. If someone reached me and said, "I need to see you for just moment after the service," I panicked.

"JESUS IS ALWAYS THERE"

In the following weeks, there were only two times I experienced total freedom from my problem, total freedom from the fear, depression, and anxiety—when I was praying or when I was preaching.

I would go up the steps of my little church to our "120 Prayer Room." We called it that because it would seat about 120 people if it were packed full. I would be alone, and I would start to pray. Each time I did this, I did not feel like praying when I began. But I would make myself do it. I would say the words to God regardless of how awful I felt.

"God, I love You."

"Lord, I thank You for what You are to me. I know You love me. I thank You for your goodness, for Your touch on my life."

At first, it was like cutting wood with a dull ax. But I had nowhere else to go, so I would keep on praying. Above all else, I would remind the Lord of His love and faithfulness, that His mercies were new every morning. It felt good to say "Great is Thy faithfulness" (Lam. 3:22-23).

Then, suddenly, He was there, and everything was all right! I know: He was *always* there. I know that now. I knew it then. What was happening was that I was momentarily free from my plaguing problem, and I was enjoying God's manifest presence, His being there.

During that time, when I was alone in the prayer room, I would sing. My father was a singer, and in my life, I have sung my way through many difficult times—pressures, problems, and fears.

I chose one song to sing more than any of the rest. It was written by Bertha Mae Lillenas in 1934, but amidst my times of depression, it became my song. I learned it in World War II when I sat in a soldier's uniform at an Assembly of God Church in Abilene, Texas. The church was pastored by one of my heroes, who became a dear friend: William A. McCann. I would sing:

Sometimes our skies are cloudy and dreary,
Sometimes our hearts are burdened with care,

But we may know, whate'er may befall us,
Jesus is always there.

There were times in that room when I would stop praying, and looking with a vacant stare at the far wall, I would ask, "God, are you *really* there?" Then the song would continue in my mind and rather softly with my voice.

"Lo, I am with you always," is written,
God will not fail to answer our prayer;
Trusting His word, we rest in His promise—
Jesus is always there.

Chorus:

Never a burden that He does not carry,
Never a heartache that He does not share,
Whether the days may be sunny or dreary,
Jesus is always there!

—"Jesus Is Always There," Bertha Mae Lillenas,
public domain

When God led me to the prayer room, and when God touched me as I was preaching, I would feel my troubles were over. There was a reason these things worked. God was showing me how to tap into the tremendous treasures of His Kingdom and His church. There was only one problem: I did not catch on to the great revelation He was offering me.

GOOD NEWS

As I have stated, my answer, my deliverance, came in one night. One moment I was living in torment and despair. Then something happened to me, and in thirty seconds, I was free. My miracle had come, and my life would be changed forever.

Keep reading, and I will tell you not only what happened but how it happened as well.

CHAPTER 2

Times of Darkness

THE FIRST OF THESE "times of darkness" came when I was only five or six years old, during the depths of the Great Depression.

My father was willing to do any kind of work. At one time, he dug ditches for seventy-five cents a day. We lived in the small town of Laurel, Mississippi.

My maternal grandfather owned a portable sawmill. He was running a large plantation in north Louisiana, cutting the timber on shares. The owner got half the money, and my grandfather got half. His whole family, except my father, mother and me, lived on the plantation and seemed to survive a lot better than we were.

My grandfather invited us to come and live with them. One of our friends in Laurel, a man by the name of Vol Sumrall, had a two-door, one-seat Model A Ford. It had what was called a "rumble seat" in the back. Some people called it a "mother-in-law" seat.

We hooked a small two-wheel trailer to the little car and moved everything we owned to Louisiana. There, Vol Sumrall sang and played a guitar. He and my dad sometimes sang together. Later, they both served as firemen. They formed a quartet called "The Laurel Firemen's Quartet."

DARKNESS IN NORTH LOUISIANA

We lived on that plantation for about one year. The name of the plantation was "Elmwood," later known as "Transylvania." The little towns of Epps, Delhi, and Lake Providence surrounded this area. With my maternal grandfather managing the plantation, we had hopes of a better life.

It was not to be. As my father quickly learned, he was not a farmer. In one year, he tried to grow and pick a bale of cotton, about 500 pounds, but he did not reach his goal. One of my mother's brothers added some cotton to what we had in order to make the bale. Another brother's large wagon took the cotton to the gin. After working for almost a year, Dad only made a few dollars when he sold the bale.

We lived in a little one-bedroom house with no electricity and no bathroom. I slept on a small bed in the living room. Although my father had no gift for farming, we didn't know what else to do. We had no place to go. We were not living; we were only existing.

And then it got worse. Darkness was all around us in the little house in Louisiana. It was a miserable existence. No one ever spoke words of encouragement. Instead, we lived with a feeling of hopelessness and despair.

CHRISTMAS ON THE PLANTATION

One event stands out in my memory. It was Christmas Eve, and my father took me with him to Lake Providence, a small Louisiana town about fifteen miles from the plantation. We rode in a cart made with two automobile wheels, pulled by the plowing mule. With the little money we had, he bought some food items we could not grow on the farm, and when he was ready to leave, he took me down the boardwalk to an old general store.

Even after all these years, I can still picture the store in my memory. The merchandise included horse collars, electrical items, plumbing materials, clothing, and foods of various kinds. But my eyes were searching for the toys.

We went to the toy department, and my dad said, "I have twenty-five cents left. I want you to pick out your Christmas present." He then showed me some items I could buy for the twenty-five cents.

I quickly spied two things I wanted. One was a large red rubber ball. The other was a jumping jack that you squeezed with your hands to make a little man do flips on an overhead bar. I bounced the ball and then squeezed the little man, making him jump. Each of them was twenty-five cents.

The little jumping man won. The store clerk wrapped him up, and I found him under the country pine Christmas tree the next morning. The decoration on the tree was colored popcorn strung on a piece of thread. We had no electricity, so there were no lights.

I did not know it, but in less than twelve months—one year—my life and the life of my parents would change forever. Light was coming!

Within one month, my grandfather, Hezekiah Edward Miller, the manager of the plantation in Louisiana, died. Then my mother's younger brother, Ernest Miller, died. He was only twenty-eight years old. He had gone to a hospital in New Orleans to have a simple surgical procedure. In the hospital, he had contracted some type of deadly viral or bacterial infection and quickly died.

In that same month, my father's mother, Mary (Molly) Green in Laurel, Mississippi, died. My father had no money for the train or bus, so he hitchhiked two hundred miles to his mother's funeral, and when he returned, my parents decided we were moving back to Mississippi.

When our family left Elmwood in Louisiana and returned to Laurel, Mississippi, I had just turned six years old. All my grandparents were dead. We made the trip back to Mississippi in the same one-seat, Model A Ford that had taken us to Louisiana only one year before. Through the years,

I learned how much Vol Sumrall and my father loved each other. Vol had taken us from Laurel to Louisiana. Now he came and brought us back.

We were back in Mississippi, but we had no money; my father had no job, and we were still in the grips of the Great Depression. At that time, I did not know the meaning of words like "sin" and "despair." But today, looking back, I realize that sin was controlling our home, and as a little boy, despair was what I felt.

CHAPTER 3

Embarrassed, Frightened, and Alone

I N September of that year, 1932, I started Prentiss School, then located on Sixth Street, between 14th and 15th Avenues. There was no kindergarten, so I started school in the first grade as a six- and-a-half-year-old little boy.

The first four months, I only went to school until noon. I do not remember any kind of teaching before that time, so on my first day at Prentiss School, I knew no letters of the alphabet. In fact, the whole process—the teaching, the class, and the social interaction—was confusing. It was like a dream. I was in it, but I did not know what part to play in the drama going on around me.

I had a horrible time trying to learn. It was difficult to concentrate on any of my schoolwork. Today, I am sure they would diagnose me with something like attention deficit disorder. My mother would sit by my side at night, hour after hour, making me repeat, over and over, the answers to the questions and problems I would face in my class.

I remember one night especially when we sat for hours going over the material I was going to face in a test the next day. When I brought my test paper home, my mother was dejected because she saw I had missed ninety percent of the answers. Every day, I hated to walk onto the school grounds.

At the same time, I could not realize what was really going on in the world. It was 1932, and the stock-market crash of 1929 meant nothing to me. I did not know that poverty, despair, and frustration had come to millions of people everywhere. All I could see were my life and the lives of my father and mother, and I thought this was the only way to live.

I had no friends. I did not visit any other children, and no child came to visit in our home.

THANK GOD FOR COMIC BOOKS

When I had a hard time learning to read, I turned to comic books. I went to the neighborhood drugstore and made a deal with the owner. Comic books cost ten cents, and since I promised to be very careful with them, he would let me take them into a back room and read each book for five cents.

Years later, just before I went into the army, I gave the kid next door two comic books. I owned the first edition of Adventure Comics where Superman was introduced. I also had the first edition of Detective Comics where Batman was introduced. I gave them away. If I had them today, those two books would be worth approximately one million dollars. That is the difference between foresight and hindsight.

I did learn to read. Years later, when I was in the army, our trip to Calcutta, India, took thirty-seven days on the Adolphus W. Greely. They had a vast library on board. I read thirty-seven books in thirty-seven days.

TEMPER AND TRIALS

During my early childhood, my parents were extremely jealous of each other. My mother was an attractive woman, and my father was a handsome man. While my father played the fiddle at country square dances, my mother would dance with different men. When my dad thought other men were making advances toward my mother, and she might be encouraging their wandering touches, he would become angry. When we got home, there would be more wild anger with curses, vile words, and threats of bodily harm. This would last throughout the night, while I retreated to the most distant corner and screamed in fear.

My father and mother both had vicious tempers. One night, a man winked at my mother while we were getting fuel at a service station. My dad jumped out of the borrowed car we were driving, grabbed a tire iron from the trunk of the car, and advanced on the man, now frightened for his life. My dad moved toward this man, cursing him and saying, "I'm going to kill you."

My mother begged Dad to stop, telling him nothing had happened. I was hysterical. I jumped from my middle seat in the old, borrowed Model A Ford, ran to my dad and begged, "Daddy, don't kill him. If you kill him, they will put you in jail, and I won't have a daddy!" I remember grabbing him by his legs while I cried and screamed at him.

Slowly, he changed. He turned, picked me up, threw the tool in the back of the car, cursed the man one final time, got in the car, and drove us away.

Though my parents often had great conflicts, I am convinced they loved each other. Many times, after their intense words and battles, I would see them the next day with tears and the words, "I'm sorry!" flowing out to each other.

STRUGGLING TO SURVIVE

I am also convinced they loved me. They worked hard to take care of me. My dad's first job that I remember was as a ditch-digger for just a few pennies a day. Later, he worked from five in the morning until noon hauling ice. Until this day, I remember his salary—once again, seventy-five cents a day.

While he was hauling ice to his customers, Dad found an old, rusty, junked truck with no wheels sitting on the ground. It was almost totally stripped, and he bought it for $4.50, paying for it in installments of fifty cents a week until he owned it.

In the next few weeks, he found a wheel here and a generator there. I sometimes rode with him in the ice truck on the later part of the mornings when I was not in school. I was with him when a lady gave him one wheel. Another time he paid twenty-five cents for another wheel and ten cents for a tire. My father, Edward Green, had a mechanical ability I do not possess. He literally rebuilt the truck with cast-off materials, using a few simple tools.

In those days, many mechanics had no regular shop, so they worked under the protection of a tree, and they became known as "shade-tree mechanics." My dad was one, and he was a good one.

When the truck was finished, Dad would go into the woods in the afternoons and cut kindling wood. People used these rich, small pieces of pine wood to start the fires in their homes. I would help him load the truck, and then we would drive up and down the streets of Laurel while I sat on top of the wood, yelling as loud as I could, "Wood for sale. . . a dollar a load." My Dad nearly always worked two jobs to help us survive.

Today, people sometimes ask me, "What do you think of the prosperity message that some people preach?" During the days of our struggle, I wish somebody had come to us with such a word. I believe I would have instantly embraced the real Bible prosperity message.

SECTION II: **A LIGHT DAWNS**

CHAPTER 4

It Happened One Night

A LL DURING THIS TIME, we were only trying to survive. In the darkness. With many questions. And no answers. And no hope.

And then it happened. On that November night in 1932, when I was still six years old, light came to our house.

After that night, nothing in our lives would ever be the same. Everything changed. It did not take a year, a month, or even a week. It happened in one night.

SUDDEN CHANGE

During my fifth and sixth years, other than the deaths of three people I loved, I remember only a few events, but they were not significant—except the jumping-jack toy I got for Christmas. I even remember the rent on our little apartment: $4.50 a month. When I use the term "significant events," I mean that nothing changed for me, for us.

But then it happened. There was no advance warning, no indication that something transformative was about to take place. No slow, discernable change came to our lives. It happened in one night. On a cold night in November of 1932, light came to our house.

And I will never forget the night that light came! Even the deaths of my two remaining grandparents did not seem significant. I had not been close to them through my short years, so I did not really understand the loss.

When we lived in Louisiana on the plantation, and when we moved back to Mississippi, my parents were not stay-at-home people. At the dances they loved to attend, there was always free food. They would eat what they wanted and then wrap up things to bring home to me, rousing me in the middle of the night: "Wake up and eat."

As I said, Dad played a fiddle—not a violin, but a fiddle. He would put it in the crook of his arm and saw away. All the people wanted him to come to their square dances, where he was the musician of the hour. He and my mother must have been the life of the parties, where there were pretty girls and handsome men. The girls seemed to like him, and the men obviously liked her—hence, the fights I witnessed after they got home.

Mom and Dad always went to someone else's home—someone who had enough money for food. They never had a dance at our little home. I hated to see them leave our apartment. I knew where they were going. I suffered with nervous palpitations of my heart, caused by fear and dread of what had happened in the past and what I feared would happen again.

But this night would be very different. In fact, it would be the most important night of their lives. It also proved to be the most important night of my six-and-a-half years of existence.

"WE'RE GOING TO BE DIFFERENT"

On this night, my parents left for what I thought was another dance. I was staying next door with a neighbor lady.

It was late, and I had gone to sleep when suddenly, my parents were there, waking me, lifting me up, and taking me out of the house. It was cold, but they were holding me close, keeping me warm. I could not fully understand what they were saying or what they were doing, but I will never forget their words.

They were both trying to carry me; they were both trying to talk to me. I did not know what their words meant, but until this day, I remember what they said. They are burned into my brain—into my very soul. We were going across a small courtyard between the two apartments, and they were crying, laughing, and talking—all at the same time. I do not remember who said which words, but the words they said changed my life forever.

"We went to church tonight. We got saved! Our life is going to be different. We are going to change."

And then my father and mother did something that will cause me to love and appreciate them even more as long as I live. They asked me to forgive them for the way they had lived, for the way they had treated each other and me. Two grown people—one thirty-six and the other twenty-six—asked a six-year-old boy to forgive them.

I do not remember what I said or how I answered them. In fact, I'm not sure I answered at all, but I do remember my amazement and wonder at what was happening. And I distinctly remember the feeling of hope that came into my life. Even now, I can take you to the place where it happened that night. It was on Fourteenth Avenue, between Fourth and Fifth Streets, in Laurel, Mississippi.

As an adult, I have returned to this place many times, to the same yard where my parents carried me and had that most important conversation. I have stood there and felt the presence of God and experienced once again the mighty, life-changing power of the Holy Spirit as I remembered that wonderful night.

Once, before that night of salvation, my mother, in a fit of anger, had attacked my father with a knife, crying out, "I'm going to kill you!" He knocked her back on the bed and took the knife from her while I screamed in the corner of the room. Many nights, I would lie in bed with my heart beating furiously, afraid a fight was going to break out at any moment.

Now, all of this was instantly over, finished. I never again heard them curse at each other. From that night, I never saw them striking blows at each other or even heard them talking about such a thing.

On that night, inside the house, they talked to each other and to me, but I did not understand what they were telling me. They seemed to be happier than ever before, and I was clinging to one statement they had made: "We're going to be different."

If they were going to be different, things had to get better, and I was glad.

CHAPTER 5

The New Light Had Come

THE NEXT MORNING, INSTEAD of arguments and harsh words, there was peace. At the breakfast table, my father took one of my hands, my mother took the other, and he prayed. As he prayed, he broke and began to weep, thanking God for our home and asking His blessing on our lives.

What I am describing is what happened to our home when the light of God's salvation came to my parents. At this time, a new musical sound also came to our home. My father was a high tenor. He became part of a Southern gospel quartet that traveled around southern Mississippi, Louisiana, and parts of Alabama, singing in churches and other auditoriums. Before the night of his dramatic conversion, he sang about Jesus because he loved the music.

Now, he sang because he loved the Savior. His new and exciting gospel singing took him to many states and into Canada.

I can still feel the difference when I hear people singing "religious" songs. I can tell whether the song is only a song or whether it comes from deep within, expressing a testimony about Jesus, a song of praise and worship to God.

Before I leave the story of my parents' conversion, I must give you the secret of their survival. Years later, as the pastor of a great church, I saw their secret in operation again when they moved from Mississippi and became a part of our church in New Orleans.

POWERFUL SERVANTS

First—my parents did not merely "get religion." They got God; Jesus came into their lives. From that night on, everything was about Jesus, the Christ—the Light of the World and the light of our lives.

Second—they instantly became servants in the house of God. They poured their lives out for the church and the people. My dad was a constant encourager to the pastor and the people of our church. While I was still young, he became the major "music man" of our little church in Laurel. We didn't call them "worship leaders" in those days. Instead, he was the "song leader."

My mother went to the homes of the sick and ministered to their needs. Many times, she would be gone all night as she sat in the hospital with those who were suffering. My parents became compassionate, tender, loving, and faithful servants of God because of the light that came to them on that November night.

They were not only servants in the little church in Mississippi, but they were the same years later when they came to our church in New Orleans. My dad had retired from the fire department in Laurel, and they had moved to Natchez, Mississippi, where he became the chief security guard for the Armstrong Tire and Rubber Company. They would drive from Natchez to New Orleans often to be in our Sunday services.

Finally, they came to our church once too often, and they were captured by the powerful presence of God. In late 1956, they moved to New Orleans. My dad became the captain of the guard for the Pinkerton Company in New Orleans, and my mom and dad were now able to regularly attend our services. Once again, they became the servants of the church. They served the people, they served me, and they served God. What a delight for our family, we who had seen the glorious light of salvation on that November night in 1932!

LIGHT CAME, AND DARKNESS FAILED

Looking back, I realize now that the devil desired to "steal, kill and destroy" the lives of Edward and Mattie Green and that six-year-old child. Satan is not omniscient, so he did not know the glorious plans God had for me, but what we must understand is this: He is out to steal, kill, and destroy every child and every family. With our family, he tried, but he failed. The light had come to erase the power of sin in our home. My parents were transformed forever!

When my parents came to God, we became faithful attendees of our little church. And we didn't just go there on Christmas and Easter. We went to church services on Sunday morning and Sunday night, prayer meeting on Tuesday night, and mid-week service on Thursday night. When a three-week revival came to our church, the Greens never missed a night.

I was happy. I now had friends. They visited in our home, and I visited in theirs. The night my parents came to Christ, I did not have one little friend. The next Sunday morning, my first time ever to go to a Sunday school, I sat on a bench with eight little boys. They became new friends who contributed so much to my life. Today, all those little friends except one are gone.

One of those little boys became my very special friend. His name was Bill Keller. He grew to become Dr. William Keller, O.D. He was the owner of the number-one optical business in Laurel for many years. Bill and I went to school together, were in the Army during World War II together, met each other in Northeast India, and came home together from the China-Burma-India Theater of Operations on the same troop ship, the *Marine Adder*, in

THE NEW LIGHT HAD COME

May of 1946. We were also best men at each other's weddings—when Bill married Ann Reynolds, and I married Barbara Self.

When the light came to banish the darkness in our home, it touched and changed every area of our lives. Christ had come to live in our house, but the church also became my life. We were blessed by our first pastor, Brother D. Frank Warren. He was a good man. When he died in 1977, I preached his funeral. To him, we owe much gratitude for bringing our family to God's glorious, eternal salvation!

HAPPY, EVEN IN "DEPRESSION"

After we found Brother Warren's thirty-by-fifty-foot sawdust-floor church, the Depression continued, but now, things were different. People had always dreamed of owning a home, driving a good car, and having nice clothes. We still did not have those things, but now we had something better—we had hope.

The Word of God gave us hope, and the songs we sang expressed our faith and gave us joy amidst pressures. One of my favorite songs as a little boy was "Come and Dine." It promised this:

Jesus has a table spread where the saints of God are fed;
He invites His chosen people, "Come and dine."
With His manna He does feed and supplies our every need
O it's sweet to sup with Jesus all the time.
"Come and dine," the Master calleth, "Come and dine."

You may feast at Jesus' table all the time.
He Who fed the multitudes, turned the water into wine,
To the hungry is calling now, "Come and dine."

—C.B. Widmyer, public domain

As I have said, my father and mother became servants to God and the church, but they also became ministers and touched thousands of lives. While my dad still worked for the fire department, he went out many weekends and preached in small country churches all over. When my parents didn't have a building in which to hold their services, they took poles and made a framework and then piled all kinds of branches and leaves on the frame to make what they called a "brush arbor."

During this time, Dad met a wonderful man named Clarence Matheny. He and his wife, Jewel, were not only saved, but they were also gloriously baptized in the Holy Spirit.

One day, Clarence was in the surgery room of a Laurel hospital. They had told him his appendix had burst, and he could not live without an immediate surgery. He was already undressed and prepped for the surgery. Then God spoke to him, "If you will go and have Edward Green pray for you, I will heal you."

Instantly, Clarence ran into his room, put on his clothes and went running down the hall, with the doctors and nurses crying out, "You can't do that."

54

But he did. He ran many blocks to the firehouse. Dad took him behind a fire truck, laid hands on him, and prayed for him, and God instantly healed him.

Later, Clarence began to preach. Many years later, he and his family moved to New Orleans and spent a year in our church. One Sunday night, he walked onto our platform, and we started this conversation:

"Brother Green, I told you I would go out to preach one day, and this is the day."

"Brother Matheny, what are you going to do about your children?"

"We are going to take them with us."

"Where are you going to go with your ministry?"

"Brother Green, we're going into all the world, like Jesus said!"

Clarence and Jewel—and their children—did go to the world: to Kenya, Tanzania, and Uganda. Before Clarence died, this couple set Africa on fire. I served as guest speaker for one of their great conferences, now run by their children, and we ministered to thousands. My father, Edward Green, had a part in this powerful ministry. Today, Clarence and Jewel Matheny's children, my dear friends, are still touching the world with the gospel of the Kingdom of God. In fact, Ronnie and Debbie Matheney are in charge of all of the Matheny ministry in Kenya; I am their pastor.

CHAPTER 6

Light and Life from Darkness and Death

WHEN I WAS IN my early teens, I walked through the front door of our little apartment one afternoon and heard my mother crying—desperately sobbing. Later, I saw her tears. I rushed to the bedroom and tried to open the door. It was locked. I pounded on the door, crying out, "What's wrong? Let me in!"

"I'M GOING TO DIE"

At first, she would not open the door. She cried out, "Go away!" I did not leave and kept asking her to let me in. Finally, the door opened. I looked at her tear-stained face, but she quickly turned away, went back to the bed, and began to sob again. Then the loud, hysterical words came tumbling out, "I'm going to die. We are poor. I'm sick; I have cancer, and we have no money for a doctor or a hospital. I'm going to die!"

I was thirteen years old. I loved my mother. I could feel her pain, but I did not know what to do, so I cried with her. If I could have only looked a few years ahead, I would have laughed. In fact, we would have had a laughing duet, for this was another time when darkness turned to glorious light.

After my mother's initial outburst, she explained her concern. She had been suffering some abdominal pain. One of her friends arranged for her to see a doctor, who told her she would have to have surgery. But we had no money for the surgery. We had no money for medicine. As far as I know, it was not possible to get medical insurance in those days, but one thing I do know—we didn't have any.

At this time, my father was working for the fire department in Laurel. The wages were low, and he still hauled wood in his homemade truck when he was not at the fire station. The Great Depression still gripped America and much of the world. At one time, we had been able to buy an old house that needed many repairs. Once we paid off the mortgage, it would be ours. But when the medical bills stacked up, it wasn't long before our home and all our money were gone. We wanted the next paycheck to come quickly.

Now, my mother was crying and saying, "I'm going to die." I sat on the edge of the bed and wept with her. When she saw my tears, she dried her own and began to comfort me. Somehow, we made it through the night until my father came home from work the next morning. What I had to tell him was not a surprise, but I told him anyway. "Dad, we have a problem."

DETERMINED TO HELP

That afternoon when my mother was crying, I knew I had to do something. We needed money. I had to help. I was thirteen years old, and it was time to go to work. There were no labor laws that prohibited a thirteen-year-old from employment, so I started looking for my first job. One of my young friends had a job with a laundry truck driver. I went to school the next day and quickly found him.

"Archie, I need a job. Can you help me get one?"

He spoke to a driver for me, and the next week, I went to work for one of the drivers for the Snow White Laundry and Cleaners. I ran from school each afternoon and met him at the laundry. From 3:30 p.m. to 6:30 p.m., he drove the truck, and I would jump out and run the laundry and dry cleaning into the homes of our customers. I did this every week, Monday through Friday.

Every Saturday, I would show up at 9:00 a.m. The driver would give me a list of our customers who had monthly accounts. I would set out on my bike to collect the money and meet the driver back at the laundry about three in the afternoon. I would turn over all the money I had collected, and then we would get in the truck and make our final deliveries. I worked twenty-four hours a week. For this, I earned two dollars a week, a little less than ten cents an hour.

One Saturday, I rode my bike and collected our money all day, and when I got back to the laundry and met my driver, I was five dollars short. Somehow, I had lost five dollars. The driver was upset, and I never knew whether he thought I had lost the money or stolen it from him. He said it was my responsibility, and I would have to pay it back.

I paid him fifty cents a week out of my two-dollar earnings, and on the Saturday when I paid the last fifty cents, I quit my job. I had never stolen anything in my life, and I would not lie to my employer. I did not want to work for anyone who thought I was a thief.

I soon got another job that paid more money. I was now fourteen years old, and my new job paid ten cents an hour. From that day until I graduated from high school, I worked forty and fifty hours a week and went to school. Most weeks, I made from four to five dollars. In those days, that was good money.

JOURNEY TOWARD CONFIDENCE

As a child, I had terrible insecurities, and as I grew into my teen years, I learned to work with people and put on a happy smile. But when I was back among my peers, I was frightfully self-conscious, feeling I would not be accepted. Until I started working for the laundry, I was shy and insecure. I could not look people in the eye when I talked. I looked down most of the time. When I was in a schoolroom, I could not get up and walk to a pencil sharpener like most students. I walked, looking down, and I had to twist my shirt collar or pull on my earlobe or my hair or rub my nose—anything to help me feel secure. It seemed to help a little.

When I started my first job, I had to learn how to deal with money. I had to talk to people at the door. Later, when I worked for a small restaurant, I had to interact more closely with the public. I learned my job, and I learned to project confidence when I walked up to the tables or ran out to their cars. But in front of any crowd, I was frightened.

FAITH FOR MY FIRST SUIT

At age fourteen, I began to grow a little, and I decided I needed a man's suit. I went down to Hamilton-Graves Clothing Store, the best men's store in town, where I found a suit that cost twelve dollars. I had a problem: I didn't have twelve dollars. So, I went to Dick Graves, one of the owners, and I introduced myself to him. I told him who I was, where I worked, how much money I made (now about four dollars a week, because I was working over 40 hours a week and making ten cents an hour) and finally, I told him what I wanted. I wanted that twelve-dollar suit. I walked out of the store with the suit, and I paid Hamilton-Graves Store fifty cents a week until my debt was paid.

After I paid for the suit, I decided I needed a new bicycle. I had been with my dad a few times in the Commercial

National Bank in Laurel, and I saw him talking to the bank president, Mr. Dwight U. Maddox. I went to Mr. Maddox and gave him the same account I had given to Dick Graves.

I was fourteen at the time, and I asked to borrow enough money from the bank to pay twenty dollars for a new bike. I asked him to make the loan to me and not tell my father. I wanted a personal loan. I figured my dad had enough financial problems without worrying about mine. I was now making twelve and a half cents an hour, or five dollars a week. I offered to pay the loan at a dollar a week.

I signed the forms, and he gave me the twenty-dollar loan. It was a few years before I learned the bank did not give me the loan. Mr. Maddox had given me the money out of his own pocket.

Twenty years later, when I was pastoring in New Orleans, I went to see Jack Livaudais, executive vice president of the Progressive Bank in New Orleans. I wanted to borrow $55,000 to buy property to build one of our church buildings. At the time, we had about 200 people in our church, but our checking account had a low balance.

I had my speech all prepared for Mr. Livaudais. When I walked into the bank, I had secured a recommendation from the former mayor of Laurel, who at the time was Lt. Governor Carroll Gartin of Mississippi. He had been my Boy Scout leader. I also had a recommendation from Mr. Dwight U. Maddox, president of the Commercial

National Bank in Laurel, the man who had given me the twenty-dollar loan to buy my bike.

Mr. Livaudais asked if I had any references. I gave him the names and phone numbers of Lt. Gov. Gartin and Mr. Maddox. I told him I had known the men since childhood and encouraged, "Ask them if I am honest—if I pay my debts and keep my word."

Within less than an hour, I walked out of the Progressive Bank in New Orleans with a commitment for a $55,000 loan. In two weeks, we had the money.

I have learned experientially that money comes to us as a result of our integrity and work ethic and the power of faith.

MY LIGHT OF SALVATION

Shortly after I started working for the laundry, A.D. Gurley, a pastor from Corinth, Mississippi, came to my hometown and pitched a gospel tent. He started a tent revival at the corner of Fifteenth Avenue and Sixth Street. He had a distinctive and impressive voice for both preaching and singing. In fact, he would have made a great Broadway actor, but his destination was not Broadway but "The Way," the Lord Jesus Christ and the Kingdom of God.

On June 22 when I was thirteen years old, under Pastor Gurley's preaching, I received Jesus into my heart and life. The old song "Victory in Jesus," written by Eugene M. Bartlett, was a new song that year. One night, a quartet composed of four pretty girls about my age sang:

O Victory in Jesus, my Savior forever

He sought me and He bought me with His redeeming blood.

He loved me e'er I knew Him, and all my love is due Him.

He plunged me to victory beneath the cleansing flood.

—"Victory in Jesus," E.M. Bartlett

I don't remember the sermon that night, but the song touched my heart, especially that part about "He loved me before I knew Him, and all my love is due Him." On that June night, kneeling at an old-fashioned altar bench, I repented of my sins and asked Jesus to come into my life and become my Lord and Savior. From that moment, even in times of great pressure, I have never felt alienated from God, and I have never doubted my salvation or His love for me.

At first, I thought I was saved because of the four pretty girls. But when the girls went back to their home in Corinth, and I still had the witness of the Holy Spirit in my heart that I was a child of God, I knew my experience was real. Over sixty years later, I was preaching an anniversary service in the Corinth, Mississippi, church and told this story while one of the girls was in the audience. (No matter how old they get, I will always call them "the girls.") We all had a good laugh over the episode.

MY MOTHER SAID, "I HAVE CANCER"

The fear of disease can be almost as bad as the disease itself. No one had ever told my mother she had cancer, but her tormenting fear would not go away. One day, one of her friends told her of a great minister who was having a revival campaign in Little Rock, Arkansas. Her friend was driving to the meeting, and she invited my mother to go with her.

When Mom got to the revival meeting, she quickly learned the rules. If she wanted to be prayed for at night, she had to attend the special teaching in a morning meeting. My mother went, got her special pass, and lined up that night for prayer.

When she reached the head of the line, the evangelist said, "Let me read your card." On the card was a place to list your problem, and my mother had written, "I have cancer." The man of God looked at her card and began to laugh!

Mom did not know what to think or do. So she waited. Then the evangelist said to her, "This is one of the great delights of my ministry. God has just spoken to me. He told me you have been listening to a lying spirit. What you have is a terrible spirit of fear concerning cancer. I am now going to pray for you, and you will be set free from this lying spirit and the fear of cancer. You will have a long life, and you will not die from cancer."

My mother, Mattie Green, was about forty-three years old when she heard this word. She lived to be eighty-eight years old, and she did not die of cancer. At home, we never talked about anyone who had cancer. But when my mother came home from her wonderful experience, she went four houses from where she lived (Mother was a practical nurse.) and cared for a lady who did have cancer. She went every day until the lady died. She never feared cancer again.

Let me leave you with an explanation and some encouraging words. My mother lived with her cancer fear for almost nine years before her day of deliverance. I have a word from the Lord for many of you who have suffered with similar problems: Don't give up! Keep on praying. Keep on believing. Help is on the way.

SECTION III: CALLED TO MINISTRY AND MARRIAGE

CHAPTER 7

Lawyer or Preacher?

WANTED TO LIVE for God, but I wanted to be a lawyer. I wanted to be the best lawyer in Mississippi. I wanted to be a United States senator. I wanted to make a lot of money. I was willing to be faithful with my tithe and offerings and to send out missionaries.

"God, You know I failed the first time I tried to speak in our church. I should have recognized that as a sign."

FACING MY FEARS

And this was true. Many people in our church had the idea that I was to be a minister, but that was certainly not my idea. Nevertheless, our pastor had asked me to speak for a year-end Watch Night service. Four young people were chosen (I was fifteen at the time.) to speak fifteen minutes each. I studied for many days, and I ended up with four pages of notes.

On the big night, when I stood up and walked to the podium, I laid my notes out before me, took one look at the congregation, and my eyes went out of focus. I quite literally could not read one word on the pages before me.

I went through what I could remember from my four pages of notes. In fact, I preached the entire Bible from what I remember, and when I finished and sat down, it had only taken five minutes. As far as I was concerned, my preaching future had ended on that night. I went home and told my mother and father, "I will never try to preach again as long as I live." But God was not finished with me.

Later in my life, it dawned on me that preaching and being a lawyer are related fields. I hope that neither preachers nor lawyers who read this book will be offended at the comparison, but I still think it is true. You must stand before the people to preach; you must also stand before the people—especially the jury—to plead your cause and your case in court.

So I did what I had often done before and would do over and over in my life—I attacked my fears. I joined the debate team in the beginning of my junior year in high school. There were twelve students on our school debating team. We made our notes on three-by-five cards. In my first debate, I stood to speak, and once again, my eyes went out of focus. I had to fearfully and frantically finish, using only what I could remember from my notes. I was ashamed, but I did not quit.

In less than nine months, I became the captain of the George S. Gardner Senior High School Debating Team in Laurel, Mississippi. I was on my way to the law career I had dreamed about.

In their leisure time, other kids might run to the football field, the baseball diamond, or the tennis court. But on the rare occasions when I was not working, I went to another court: the Jones County Circuit Court. I sat in on every courtroom case possible and listened with fascination as the lawyers argued on behalf of their clients. I watched the proceedings and listened to the words of the judges with great awe.

I got to know one judge so well that he would take me into his chambers after court adjourned for the day and talk to me about the law. When he ran for reelection, I went into the neighborhoods, stood on a wood crate, pushed beyond my fears, and made political speeches for him. His name was Judge Pack. He won the race by a landslide.

THE BIRTH OF HOPE

But fear had been instilled in me as a child. When I had those experiences of failure in school, when I could not remember anything I read and little of what I heard, I came to feel I was inferior to the other normal students. My parents also felt under condemnation for the past mistakes in their own lives, and they did not know how to help me with my insecurities. In fact, my mother felt fear was positive. She felt that the more I feared, the more I would try to learn.

When I tried to speak and was paralyzed with fear, it only confirmed what I had felt. As a child, I could feel alone in the middle of a crowded room. In every crowd, it was "them" and "me." I felt as if I were far back in a deep tunnel, looking out at the world through a long hollow pipe. I could see what was going on, but I was not a part of it. That's the way I felt on my first day of school and many times afterward.

I was able to partially recover when I went to work in the ice cream store, but it was not until I joined the debating team that my life really changed. Hope began to be born in me. I did have a brain. I could do it if I tried.

In my freshman year of high school, I passed with Ds and a few Cs. In my sophomore year, I made all Cs. As a junior, I made Bs. And, in my senior year, I worked a thirty-hour week and made straight As. But I still had not resolved the dilemma about becoming a preacher or lawyer. Deep down, I hoped law would prevail.

CHAPTER 8

Embracing the Ministry

I HAD KNOWN I was called to the ministry since I was sixteen years old. Some of my friends and I had attended an old-fashioned camp meeting in the northeast corner of Mississippi, in Tishomingo County. Many of the people were there to receive and enjoy the blessings of God. I was there to see my friends and to take a vacation from my work. I stayed away from many of the services.

FAR FROM GOD

At this point in my life, I really felt far from God. I was working hard and putting in many long hours. I was going to church only on Sunday mornings, and I had begun to sit closer to the back of the auditorium instead of near the front.

The final night of the camp meeting came, and I was sitting on a bench in the middle of the grounds, listening to my Zenith portable radio. It was advertised as an "international radio" with regular channels and short-wave channels that brought in sounds from all over the world. It was my reward to myself. My radio had long-life batteries, and it weighed eleven pounds. When I carried it around, I usually set it up on my shoulder so I could hear the music while I was walking.

Sitting on the bench with my radio at my side, I was listening to the Glen Miller Orchestra playing one of its big hits, "In the Mood."

Suddenly, a man was standing by me. I looked up to see Rev. Howard Goss, one of the pioneers of our church movement and one of the founders of the worldwide General Council of the Assemblies of God. He was standing over me, asking, "Aren't you going to the service?"

"I don't think so. I think I'm going to my cabin."

He told me, "No, go put your radio in your cabin and come back here. I will wait for you, and we will go together." I respected him highly, and I quickly complied.

After the songs were over and the preaching began, I left the big tent and stayed outside, leaning against a tree safely covered by the darkness. I could see into the tent, but no one inside could see me. I wanted to be careful that I did not get too close and too involved with all that was going on.

At the end of the preaching under the tent on that Mississippi night, the preacher invited people to come down for prayer—for salvation or for any need in their life. For a while, I watched from my safe covering.

Suddenly and without any forethought, I started to walk into the big tent. I did not stop at the edge; I kept walking until I was right in the middle of all the people who had gone up to the front for prayer.

I stood there for a moment, and my thoughts were racing. *I'm not living right; I'm far from God. What am I going to do?* I decided to kneel. When my knees touched the sawdust-covered ground, God instantly touched me. In a moment, I was praying and rejoicing as the presence of God enveloped me. I don't know how long I was there, but when I stood up, I knew!

I knew, as I had never known before, that God loved me.

I knew I had been restored to a right relationship with God.

And I knew God had called me into the ministry. I was not happy about it, but I knew it. I did not immediately tell anyone what had happened to me there. My mother was present in the camp meeting, and she questioned me about my going forward. I told her as little as possible, but I knew that she knew.

LEARNING ABOUT GOD'S GRACE

The major thing that happened to me that night was that I received a revelation of the grace of God. I knew I had done nothing to "get back to God." I had been taught that when people wander away from Him, they must go to the altar and cry out in repentance and then *beg* God to forgive them. Sometimes this would take many long sessions of prayer.

I found this idea untrue. The instant I moved toward God, He saw my heart, knew my need, and instantly touched my life, giving to me the warmth of a refreshing relationship.

I learned that night that we do not receive anything from God because we are "worthy," but because Christ is worthy—and we are in Christ. We once sang a chorus in our church that said this:

There's nothing more that I can do, for Jesus paid it all,
And we are complete in Him.

—"Complete in Him," author unknown

Through the years, I have experienced the peace and power of God's "Amazing Grace." The songwriter had a great revelation when he penned these words:

Through many dangers, toils and snares, I have already come;
'Tis grace that brought me safe thus far, and grace will lead me home.

Never again would I be afraid to approach God, ask His forgiveness, and seek His help. That is why, years later, when I was in the middle of my battle with fear and torment, I was never afraid to go to God. I loved God; I trusted God. That is why I would find peace in the prayer room and feel the joy of His presence when I preached.

IN THE ARMY

But after that wonderful camp meeting night when I was sixteen years old, I did not start preaching. I wanted to be a lawyer who would help other people go out and preach.

In the early morning hours of June 6, 1944, I heard the voice of the young man who delivered our daily newspaper. With his loudest voice, he was yelling: "Extra, extra! American troops have landed on Omaha Beach in France! Extra, extra! The invasion of Europe has begun!" He was announcing the Allied invasion of France during World War II.

I quickly threw on my robe, ran to the door, and bought a newspaper. I then went to one of my last days of school before graduation. We did nothing but listen to the radio all day. I came home, and we listened again through the night until the early morning.

Within eleven days, I found myself at Camp Shelby, Mississippi, being inducted into the United States Army. I did my basic training in Camp Barkley, Texas, close to Abilene.

After my basic training was finished, I set out to find a good church. I'd heard about a great preacher in Abilene. I walked into his Assembly of God Church in Abilene, Texas, and heard the people singing this old song, written in 1929 by C. Bishop. He had read the parable of Jesus telling the story of the prodigal son. He wrote this great song that seemed to tell the story of my relationship with God:

Verse 1:

That God should love a sinner such as I,
Should yearn to change my sorrow into bliss,
Nor rest 'till He had planned to bring me nigh,
How wonderful is love like this!

Chorus:

Such love, such wondrous love,
Such love, such wondrous love,
That God should love a sinner such as I,
How wonderful is love like this.

Verse 4:

And now He takes me to His heart—a son,
He asks me not to fill a servant's place;
The far-off country wand'rings all are done,
Wide open are His arms of grace!

— "That God Should Love a Sinner Such as I,"
C. Bishop, R. Harkness

When I first went to the Abilene Assembly of God Church, I was eighteen, and the young pastor, Bill McCann, was twenty-nine. We stayed in touch until his death in 2015 at the age of ninety-nine.

Just ten months after I joined the army, I was on a troop ship, headed for Calcutta, India, then on into Central Burma. I was stationed with a supply depot on what was called "The

Burma Road." We were at the halfway point between Ledo, India, and Kunming, China.

We furnished medical and quartermaster supplies to troops fighting in Southeast Burma and Southwest China. While in Myitkyina, Burma, I got a little ribbon with a star on it to indicate that I was serving in a battle zone even though the only enemies I ever saw were prisoners of war. I ended up in an administrative supply group and not the infantry for only one reason: In high school, I had learned to type sixty-five words a minute.

The army had special courses we could attend two nights a week. While in Burma, I took the jeep and drove through part of the jungle area to attend pre-law courses. The ministry remained somewhere in the back of my mind, but I tried not to think about it.

FEAR OF FLYING

When I was eight years old, an old Ford Tri-Motor airplane came to Laurel. The plane landed on a grass-covered runway. My mother took me to see it. When we got there, she learned they would take passengers for a short ride for fifty cents per person. She gave them one dollar, and she and I went up with about a dozen other passengers.

The first time the plane did a steep bank, I was terrified and began to scream with fear. My mother held me close and tried to calm me. I stopped crying, but the fear remained.

Eleven years later, as a nineteen-year-old serviceman, I was in the town of Ledo, India. One night, they told us we would be leaving the next morning, flying to Myitkyina, Burma, for our next assignment. The whole night was horrible for me. Just the thought that I was going to have to fly again brought a feeling of terror.

The next morning, they took us by army truck to the Ledo airport where we were loaded into an Air Force C-47 airplane. (The civilian designation for this plane is the DC-3.) We had sixteen passengers on the plane.

My heart was pounding. I wondered if this were the day I was going to die. I watched the high Himalayan Mountains as we passed through them—not over them. When the plane banked in one direction, I leaned the other way. It was 120 minutes of deep anxiety before we landed in Myitkyina.

Four months later, we flew back from Myitkyina to Ledo. Nothing had changed. I was still afraid to fly.

HEARING GOD'S VOICE

Finally, the war was over, and I was home. But instead of being happy, I was filled with unrest. I was ready to get into college and start training for my law career, but the inner voice kept saying something different.

In the middle of the night, I was suddenly wide awake. I had heard a voice calling: "Wake up, Charles, I am calling you."

Are some of the guys in the neighborhood playing games with me? I went to the window and looked out to see if anyone were there. Of course, I saw no one. A few nights later, it happened again. I was once again fully and instantly awake. I went to my parents' bedroom and quietly looked in. They were sleeping.

At that moment, I remembered the way God had called Samuel in the Bible, speaking to him in the nighttime. Samuel went back to his bed and said, "Speak Lord, for your servant is listening" (see 1 Sam. 3:10).

I did not say that.

I just went back to bed and thought about it with much frustration.

A few days later, I finally made up my mind that I would go to a Christian university, Bob Jones University in Greenville, South Carolina, for my first two years of college and then transfer to Louisiana State University for my law training.

When I got to Bob Jones, I did not commit myself to the ministry. But after only a few weeks, another sudden event occurred.

I was in a morning chapel service, and Jesse Hendley, a Baptist minister from Atlanta, Georgia, was preaching. Until this day, I do not remember what he said that reached into my heart, but I do know God used him and his words to end my indecision and totally change my plans for my future life.

When the chapel service was over, I did not go to my next class. I went back to my dormitory room, closed the door, got down by my bed and began to talk to God: "The struggle is over. For whatever my life is worth to You, from this moment, I am Yours. I will go where You want me to go; I will do what You want me to do."

I did have one small reservation left, however. I felt that if God did not open the door of ministry, I would be free to become a lawyer. I got up and walked out the door with my books in my hand, headed for my class. As I walked across the campus, one of my new friends was walking in a diagonal pattern, coming toward me. As we met, he said, "Charles, I have been meaning to ask you a question. What are you going to be? What are you going to do with your life?"

I was amazed. Five minutes before, I had made a private commitment to God. I began to smile, and then I laughed and quickly said to him, "I'm going to be a preacher!" It felt good. And I realized what God had done in me. He not only wanted my private commitment concerning the ministry; He wanted my "word confession" to my friend—to the world—concerning my dedication to the Kingdom of God. Since that day, I have known that everything is really settled when we "believe in [our] heart and confess with [our] mouth" (Rom. 10:9b, NKJV).

By the way, I have stayed so busy in the ministry I have never found time to go to law school.

CHAPTER 9

From Preacher to Pilot

TWO WEEKS AFTER I surrendered to the ministry, the university announced a sermon contest. The idea was to write a doctrinal sermon that could be preached in fifteen minutes. Seven hundred other students and I entered. The subject of my sermon was the cross. Judges would choose twenty-four students out of the seven hundred to enter the final phase of the contest.

One of my roommates was a junior, and he quickly let me know I was wasting my time. "You are only a freshman," he said. "This school is twenty-five years old. No freshman has ever been chosen in the top twenty-four."

But somehow, the guy who didn't want to preach, the one who had trouble learning—yes, I became the first freshman in the school's history to make it into the final twenty-four.

I also entered the school with no college credits. Two years and nine months later, I graduated with 132 semester hours and a baccalaureate degree—double majors in religion and English, minors in history, speech, and New Testament Greek.

I'm not really that intelligent. What brought me through these months was perseverance and the confidence that God was with me. I felt in my heart that I would not, could not fail.

I still had some fears about "this preaching thing." I was afraid no one would want me, that I would have nowhere to go, no place to preach. So I preached everywhere. I went to a jail in Athens, Tennessee, and preached to the prisoners. I went to homes for the elderly. I preached on the street in Greenville, South Carolina (once, in the rain), and in many other Tennessee and Carolina towns. In fact, while I was in college, I preached somewhere at least once a week.

During this time, I almost got in trouble while preaching in the Athens, Tennessee, jail. The jailer put me in what they called the "bull pen," with the cells all around me. Some prisoners were sleeping while others played cards. I said to them, "Fellows, if I were a lawyer, I would tell you how to plead your case, but to tell the truth, I have come to tell you how to escape."

Now I had their undivided attention, so I quoted Hebrews 2:3a (KJV): "How shall we escape if we neglect so great salvation?"

I am so glad the jailer did not hear me.

AN OLD FEAR REVISITED

When the army experience ended and I went on to college, the fear of flying remained with me. I hated to think about ever doing it again. Then one day in a chapel meeting, the dean made an announcement.

"Tomorrow, we will begin an aviation program in our school."

I left the chapel, but the words of the announcement did not leave my mind. I sat on a concrete bench on one of the walkways, and I began to talk to myself. *This is going to be an "air age," and you cannot be left out. You must conquer this fear!*

That night, before I went to bed, I made up my mind. I would not run from my fear of flying any longer. I would confront it and attack it.

The next morning, I was one of the first people in line to sign up for flight training. The following day, I showed up at the airport in Greenville, South Carolina, for my first flying lesson. I met my instructor in the "ready room," and we walked together to the airplane. It was a small yellow J-3 Piper Cub with tandem seats. He sat in the front seat, and I was in the rear.

In the ready room, I had noticed a sign on the wall. It stated, "There are old pilots and there are bold pilots; but there are no 'old bold pilots.'" When I read those words, I thought, *I will never be a "bold" pilot.*

We sat in the plane on the ground before my instructor started the engine, and he showed me the controls. The front panel had an altimeter, an airspeed indicator, an artificial horizon, a heat gauge, and other devices that communicated information. To my left, about waist high, was the throttle, which I was to operate with my left hand. The rudder pedals and the "land brakes" were positioned so I could operate them with my feet. For my right hand, there was the "stick" that helped to control the airplane in flight. He did a great job of explaining, and I was desperately trying to listen despite the loud voices of fear exploding in my mind.

"You line up the plane on the runway. You push the throttle forward, and the plane will start rolling. As soon as you get some speed, you push the stick forward, and it will raise the tail off the runway. You keep an eye on your speed, and when it gets to about sixty-five miles an hour, pull back gently on the stick, and you will begin to fly."

My instructor explained all this before starting the engine. When he was finished with these basic instructions, he said with a smile, "Let's fly this airplane."

The plane had no electric starter, so he had a young man "pull the prop." With the second pull, the engine started. We began to taxi out to the runway. The instructor told me to follow through with him on the controls. I seized the stick with both hands as if it were a snake I was trying to crush.

He quickly felt what I was doing and began to push the stick violently from side to side. Whatever he did to the stick with his hand also happened to mine. He was beating my legs, so I quickly let loose of my stick. He took off, and for the next ten minutes, he allowed me to use only one finger on top of the stick to show me how easy it was to control the airplane.

As the little Cub lifted into the air, I wished with all my heart I were back on the ground. *Why did I do this? This isn't going to work. I will never learn to fly an airplane!*

But I did. Eleven weeks from that day, I was flying the little J-3 Piper Cub solo at five thousand feet, doing tail spins, practicing for my check ride to qualify for my private pilot's license. The FAA doesn't require this anymore for private pilots, but when I learned to fly, you had to demonstrate your ability to fly the plane in and out of a spin.

When I pulled out of that first solo spin and was flying straight and level, I began to laugh like a crazy man—but a happy one. My fear of flying was gone! I had attacked my fear and conquered it.

My instructor told me, "You are a natural-born pilot. You can really feel it, can't you?" I learned how to take off and land on short strips. When I was flying, I felt like I was a part of the plane.

NO MORE FEAR

Since then, I have traveled on commercial flights in the middle of typhoons in the South China Sea and in violent weather all over the world. I was on a Delta 757 when an engine exploded fifteen seconds off the ground. As the plane lurched, my seatmate (a first-time flyer) grabbed my arm in fear. I smiled at her and said, "It's going to be all right. This is a good plane. It can fly on one engine. Don't be afraid; we're going to make it." And we did.

Not long ago, I was flying as a passenger in a twin-engine King Air plane. We only had one pilot, and he asked me if I would like to come up and sit in the co-pilot's chair. Of course I did. I stayed with him for about five hundred miles, asking many important questions: "Where are the flaps? What is the glide speed? How do you work the radio? Where is the landing gear lever?" And so it went.

By the time I walked back to the passenger compartment, I felt confident that if I had to, I could land the airplane, though I have never flown a multi-engine plane. In fact, every time I get on a huge 747, I look out the window as we are taking off, and think, *If something happened—if they needed me, I think I could fly this thing.*

If that ever happened, I suppose the other passengers would have to confront their fears.

CHAPTER 10

From Pilot to Pastor

I HAD LEARNED TO conquer my fear of flying, but God still had some things He wanted to teach me as a young student minister. One Monday morning, a classmate came to me with a wonderful possibility. About one hundred miles south of Greenville, South Carolina, is the city of Augusta, Georgia. In Augusta, Grover Langston was pastor of the First Assembly of God. He wanted an assistant who could help him with the music and the youth of his church.

A MINISTRY POSITION

My friend had told Pastor Langston about me, and the pastor sent his telephone number, requesting that I call him if I were interested in the job. I called him that night. We arranged that I would go to Augusta on Friday afternoon after my last class. I arrived at the bus station in Augusta just as it was getting dark. The pastor picked me up and took me to his home.

He talked at length about his church and about what he was looking for in an assistant. Then he asked me many questions. The next morning at the breakfast table, he announced that he wanted me to take the job, and he set up certain rules for our relationship.

First, I was *not* to be the assistant pastor but his personal assistant. I had no relationship with the church but only with him.

His church was the First Assembly of God in Augusta. (There were two more Assemblies of God churches in the city.) He did not mind that I did not belong to the denomination, but I agreed not to announce that fact to anyone in the congregation.

I was to take care of the music ministry for the Sunday services, morning and night. I would also direct the choir and lead the congregation in singing.

I would get to Augusta every Friday afternoon and be in charge of the youth service on Friday nights. About twice a month, I would also preach in the Sunday-night service.

We agreed on all these points, and I was hired and began immediately. The next three and a half months were a delight to me. I liked the pastor and the people of the church, and they were actually paying me! Not much, but I did get paid.

A BIG CHANGE

One weekend when I arrived at the Langston home, Grover took me into his study and told me he was leaving the church and going to Atlanta to pastor a larger church. Two days later, on Sunday, he made that announcement to the church.

The people were stunned. No one said anything to me, and that night, I packed up and went back to the university as usual.

The following Sunday morning, I went to the university service. About three in the afternoon, someone said there was a telephone call for me. I went down two floors in my dorm and picked up the phone. The secretary-treasurer of the church, a deacon named Rabun Scott, was on the phone. This is how our conversation went:

"Where were you this morning?"

"I was here, on the campus."

"We expected you to be here and preach in the church today."

"No one told me that."

"Well, we want you to be our new pastor."

I did not think this was possible. Also, the church had some serious divisions, and I wasn't sure I wanted to deal with that. However, we continued our conversation.

"I can't be your pastor. I don't belong to the Assemblies of God."

"We don't care about that. We want you. What will it take to get you to come and pastor this church?"

Thinking quickly, I came up with what I thought were two impossible conditions. I said, "I will come and be your pastor if two things happen."

"What are those things?"

"Tonight, you will call a business meeting for Wednesday night. If I am elected unanimously (I was safe; they had never done anything unanimously.), and if the state superintendent of the Assemblies of God for the state of Georgia will call or write, giving me permission to take the church, then I will become your pastor."

The following Thursday morning, I received a call telling me I had been unanimously elected pastor of the First Assembly of God in Augusta, Georgia. The next day, I received a special delivery letter from Superintendent Jones from the state office. I can still remember the main part of his letter. He wrote, "I have investigated you; I believe in you, and I believe you will help bring this church together. We will give you all the assistance possible. Take it, and God bless you." The church did not split but became one in the Lord.

ANOTHER PASTOR

However, I was scheduled to graduate from Bob Jones University in four months, and I did not believe God was calling me to live in Augusta and be the church's permanent pastor. I attended a Christ's Ambassadors service (youth meeting) in Macon, Georgia, where I met a young minister by the name of Joe Westbury. I did not hear him preach; I only heard him pray. It was a fantastic, Holy Spirit-anointed prayer.

I was looking for a new pastor for my church, and I went to Joe after the service and asked, "Would you consider becoming the pastor of the First Assembly of God in Augusta?"

His instant answer was a firm "Yes."

Three weeks later, he came to Augusta and preached a great message on Sunday morning and another on Sunday night. I still remember the title of his Sunday-morning message and the words of Jesus he used: "But if I with the finger of God cast out demons, no doubt the kingdom of God has come upon you" (Matt. 12:28).

After he preached Sunday night, I sent him out of the auditorium, conducted a business meeting, and then brought him back in. I announced to him in front of the congregation, "You have been unanimously elected as the new pastor of the First Assembly of God."

I said goodbye to the church and to my friends, Rabun and Alma Scott. I walked out of the church, went to the bus station, and left Augusta. To this day, I have never been back to that city.

Joe Westbury went on to become a great pastor. He also started a nursing home business in the city of Augusta that became a huge financial success. With a generous and joyful heart, he supported missionaries all over the world with large sums of money.

CHAPTER 11

A Light Called Barbara

OMING OUT OF COLLEGE, I preached during that first summer in Houston, Texas. I was invited to a church for one week and stayed seven. The pastor offered me a job as his associate, but I was already "promised." Pastor W. H. Marshall had offered me a job in Baton Rouge, Louisiana. He had been my pastor in Mississippi for three years, and after he had moved to Baton Rouge when I was sixteen, we stayed in close touch.

I went to Baton Rouge, lived in the pastor's home, became his associate—and also attended the graduate school of Louisiana State University. I was working on an advanced degree in the field of English. I was making thirty-five dollars a week.

SURPRISE VISIT

A Greyhound bus had brought me from Houston to Baton Rouge at the end of August, 1949. Pastor Marshall and his family were on vacation, and one of their friends, Paul Lowenberg, was supplying for them. Brother Lowenberg and I had met one time before, but on that day, we became friends. He went on to be one of the bright stars of the Assemblies of God, becoming a lifetime honorary member of the General Board and at times preaching on their national radio program. I loved him and his dear wife, Bernice, for the rest of their lives.

But on that day in 1949, Pastor Lowenberg met me at the bus station and announced two things. We were going to visit a patient in Our Lady of the Lake Hospital, and then we were going to the Piccadilly Cafeteria to eat lunch.

"Who is the patient?" I asked.

"Her name is Barbara Self. She had an appendectomy."

I knew Barbara Self. I had met her two years earlier when I preached for Pastor Marshall while on a college break. An interesting thing had happened. That Sunday morning, she had sung a solo. She had a great voice, I liked the song, and she was a pretty girl. That night, I had preached.

UNFORGETTABLE

That Sunday night, we were back at the pastor's home, having a late snack. The phone had rung, and Mrs. Marshall (Mary) had come back and said, "Charles, it's for you."

I went to the phone and said, "Hello." It was little Barbara Self.

"I wanted to call and tell you I enjoyed your message."

"Thank you, Barbara; I enjoyed your song."

Charles' and Barbara's engagement photo (1950)

"I know you were busy and probably didn't have a chance to get my phone number and address, so I thought I would call and give it to you."

I said, "Thank you, Barbara, let me write it down."

I did, but she was so young—pretty and a good singer—but young.

I never did call her, but I had never forgotten her.

That morning, Paul Lowenberg and I walked into Barbara's hospital room.

She looked at me and said, "Charles Green, what are you doing here?"

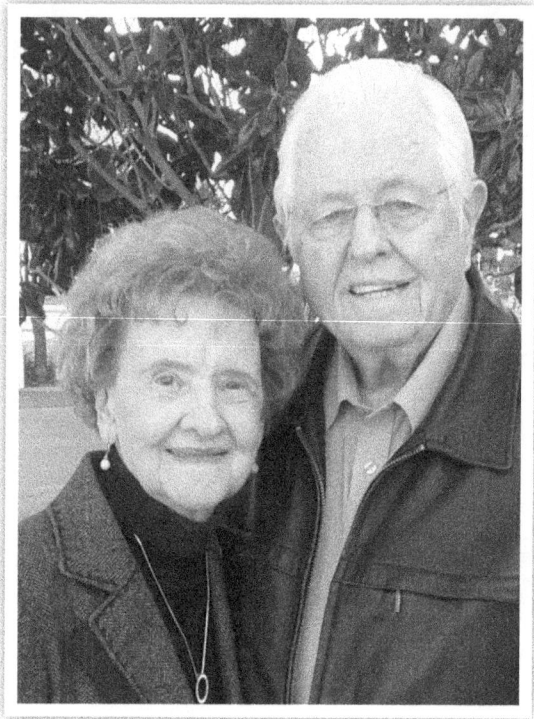

Charles and Barbara in 2015

I smiled at her and said, "I came to hold your hand."

Dramatically, she held out her hand. I walked across the floor, took her hand, and held it for a few minutes while we talked, and then I prayed for her.

Five months and seventeen days from that hospital visit, Barbara and I were married. On thirty-five dollars a week! We had a lot of faith—not much money, but a lot of faith.

She had been told by some of the people around her, "Charles is flighty. He will not stay with you six months."

We laughed about that.

On the morning of our fiftieth wedding anniversary, I punched Barbara on the arm to wake her up. Very sleepily she said, "What do you want?"

"Do you know what day this is, Barbara?"

"Yes, it is our fiftieth anniversary."

"I have a question for you."

"What's the question?"

"I want to know, are you beginning to have more confidence in the permanence of this marriage?"

"Charles, you are still crazy."

MIKE SELF

Barbara Jean Self Green became the light of my life through all the years. But it was that telephone call—the one when she called to give me her address and phone number—that did it. That made it happen. I could never get her out of my mind.

On the same day I visited Barbara in the hospital, I met her dad for the first time. He was one of the managers of the Piccadilly Cafeteria. Pastor Lowenberg and I were walking down Third Street (the main street in Baton Rouge,

Louisiana), getting ready to turn into the cafeteria when John Leonard (Mike) Self came walking out.

This wonderful man became my father-in-law, my dear friend and finally an elder in our church in New Orleans. He was one of the greatest, sweetest men of God I have ever known.

Years later, when Barbara and I started the church in New Orleans, we didn't have much money. We usually spent two days a week in Baton Rouge. We told people we were going to see her mom and dad, but we were really going to eat at the Piccadilly. We owe a great debt to Piccadilly, to founders T.H. Hamilton and his son-in-law, Bill Richards—and to Mike Self for feeding us many times in those difficult days.

In the beginning, I thought the food was "on the house." Then I found out the most honorable Mike Self would take money out of his pocket and put it in the cash register to pay for our meals. He was truly a godly and gracious man.

SECTION IV: **DELIVERANCE COMES**

CHAPTER 12

My Four Big Fears

A FTER BARBARA AND I had been married twelve years, we found ourselves pastoring a small church in Port Arthur, Texas. We started with thirty-seven people. Within three months, we had two hundred. We stayed in Port Arthur for two years. Afterward, we traveled and preached all over Europe for almost a year.

In New Orleans, we started with ten people. When we had about fifty people, we received building-fund offerings and borrowed money from the bank. Shortly afterward, construction started on our first building. It was fifty by one hundred feet, with a small balcony in the rear of the auditorium that we used for classrooms. That upstairs area was our youth auditorium and our prayer room too where, as I mentioned, I would go when the powers of darkness almost overwhelmed me. It was the place where I found help. I still believe in prayer for many reasons, but the main reason? It works.

As a thirty-five-year-old pastor who found himself afraid of many things, I stood at my back door and asked God about my *real* problem. I insisted on an answer! Turning around, I walked to the kitchen table, switched on a dim light, sat myself down, and began to write. I listed those fears.

THE FOUR BIG FEARS

1. **I'm afraid about our church.** At that time we had less than one hundred people, and they were poor. We were operating on a budget of two hundred dollars a week. Out of that, we paid our mortgage, the utilities—electricity, gas, and water—and all the other miscellaneous bills that come with running a ministry. Our family—we now had Michael and Cynthia—lived on the rest.

When any of our members confronted me about a problem, my first thought was, *They are going to leave the church*—with their money. It is a terrible thing for a minister to look to people as his source. I had not yet received the revelation that God is the source. I was still operating under the assumption that our church's financial well-being depended on its people, and I was afraid concerning our lack of finances.

When I couldn't sleep at night, I often wracked my brain to assure myself that I had not offended anyone during the previous few days. Every casual word required deep rumination, and if there were any possibility of offense, I had to mend the relationship instantly.

2. I'm afraid I can't take care of my family. Our church did not have a medical plan for the first nineteen years of its existence, yet God took care of our every need. We—the church or our family—never had a bill that was overdue beyond thirty days, but personal finances became one of my plaguing fears. My constant attitude was "Sure, we made it last month, but what about the future?"

When our church had about a hundred people, and my salary was up to a hundred dollars a week, Barbara and I decided it was time to build a house. We had found a lot on which to build in the middle of an old cow pasture. The city was adding streets, and the lots sold for $750.00. We bought our lot, and as soon as the city laid the street, we started to build. I served as my own contractor, and some of the church members were my crew.

We moved into our house for a cost of $18,000—including the cost of the lot. The payments were $186 a month, and I fretted daily that we would not meet next month's payment. The fact that we had never missed one did not seem to calm my emotions. I was still fearful. I sold the house about three years later. You can imagine my chagrin when I learned that over time those lots had risen in value to $100,000 each. Now I wish I had bought more and saved them!

3. I'm afraid something bad is going to happen to one of my children.

There was no reason for this fear, but fear is not reasonable! Every time I left the house, I gave Barbara careful instructions regarding the children. "Don't let them play by the street. A car will kill them. Don't let them go near any body of water. They will drown." And so it went. She feared because of my fears, and I regret that.

I have been asked, "Was there something in your background, your history, that caused you to fear for your children's lives?" If there were anything of that nature, I never found it. To me, it was just another means by which the devil used to plague me.

Finally, I wrote down the last one.

4. I wasn't afraid of death, but despite all I had said to the contrary, I *was* afraid I was going to die and leave my family with nothing.

There is a difference. I wasn't afraid for my sake that I was going to die, but I was afraid of what would happen to my family—Barbara, Michael, and Cynthia—and to the church if I were to die as a young husband, father, and pastor.

I even had the fear of *how* I was going to die—what was going to kill me. Like my mother, I believed it would be cancer. And I was sure it was already growing in my body. On my right side, a painful lump, a knot, was located. To touch it was as excruciating as touching one's eyeball. When friends would greet me with enthusiasm, they would sometimes grab me on both sides, touching that place, and I would feel like screaming. I felt that sooner or later, probably sooner, that lump was going to be the cancer that would kill me. I suppose it was a case of "Like mother, like son."

After I had documented my four big fears on paper, I got up from the table. I walked back to that kitchen window and gazed out into the darkness. The taunting words of Satan and my own negative imagination began to harass me. "Who told you to do this preaching thing? Don't you remember how insecure and timid you were as a child. This time, it's worse. There is more at stake. You should have quit the first time you tried to speak to a congregation, the time you 'froze' and failed."

There was just enough truth mixed with all the lies to make it a confusing accusation. I have learned that when you mix a lie with truth, the whole thing becomes a lie. Condemnation and a negative attitude stayed with me like a stain that could not be washed out of a garment. At times, I felt like scolding God: "I told you I didn't want to be a preacher. Other young people were sitting on the edge of the pew with their Bibles in their hands, anxiously waiting to rise up and answer the call. Why didn't you send *them* to this town of New Orleans?"

CHAPTER 13

"You Are a Preaching Machine"

MENTIONED THERE WERE two activities that brought me relief, and one of them occurred in the prayer room, when it was just God and me. The other time was when I was preaching to our church. I would begin my message as if I were a machine. I knew how to do it. One man had even told me, "You are a preaching machine!" Now, I was demonstrating that ability. I would start the message without any feeling at all. I just turned myself on and commenced. The people expected me to do it. I was a preacher, and I was going to do just that. I knew the drill. I knew the words, and I would say them.

"God is a good God. He is here to help you. Jesus is the Healer, and He will meet your need. God's Word is powerful. Believe it, act on it, and you will have everything you need. Trust God with your life. He will take care of you."

I said it all. And, to the best of my ability, I believed every word. But I still struggled.

In our church, and in my ministry, people would believe the Word, come to Christ, and receive His salvation. They would get healed. That sequence of events occurred for everyone it seemed—but me. I continued to preach what I honestly believed was the Word of God, but at the beginning of each sermon, I felt like a vending machine delivering a product. Then *it* would happen. About five or ten minutes into my message, the anointed touch of God would come upon me. I could feel the presence and power of the Holy Spirit, and at that moment, my words would begin to flow, and every dark cloud would disappear.

I remember one Sunday morning when this happened. I was preaching the Word of God, and at the same time I was thinking, *It's over. I'm delivered. Everything is going to be all right.* The message ended, the service concluded, and finally Barbara and I walked to our car. I got in and started the engine. I placed my hands on the steering wheel, and suddenly, they began to shake. I looked at Barbara, "You will have to drive. I can't do it."

QUESTIONS I COULDN'T ANSWER

I couldn't sleep that Sunday night, and at 3:00 a.m., I was out of bed, standing in the middle of the room. Barbara was also awake. This had gone on long enough that I had attempted to tell her what was happening to me.

This time, she had a question for me: "Are you afraid?"

"I suppose I am. Yes, I know I am."

"What are you afraid of? Are you afraid you might die?"

For the first time in weeks, I laughed. I told her, "The thought of dying is the only thing that keeps me going."

Throughout this entire period, I had fought the battles of hell, but I had *never* considered suicide. Nevertheless, the thought of dying was pleasant. It brought relief. Before I flew in an airplane, I would buy a huge insurance policy. If any airplane were going to fall, I wanted to be on it. Then I would be free of my struggle, and my family would have the funds they needed for a good life. It seemed like a win-win.

GOD WAS SHOWING THE ANSWER, BUT I COULDN'T SEE IT

While all my anxieties, uncertainties, and agonies continued, God started providing some answers. There were clues all along the way. I just could not see them.

I kept asking Barbara, "What am I going to do?"

I rejected every answer she suggested—except one. I decided to share my dilemma with my dear friend, Garlon Pemberton. He was pastoring a church on the Mississippi Gulf Coast, and other than my wife, he knew me like no other person. Garlon and I had been through many difficult times together. I had walked with him through many of his battles. Now, I decided it was time for him to trod with me.

What a wise decision that was! From that moment, Barbara and I were not alone. Garlon was with me through the remaining experience. We prayed together. He called me on a regular basis, and his words were always encouraging.

"God is with you. He is going to bring you through this thing."

Just hearing him say it made me feel better. But the problem was not solved.

Another night, as I walked the floor wringing my hands in frustration, I could feel the darkness closing in on me. For some reason, at that moment, I began to retrace the steps of my life. I began to search my mind concerning my past struggles. It was then I realized this was not the first time I had dealt with this feeling of hopelessness and despair. Night after night, in my memories, alone in the darkness, I reviewed my life.

Slowly I began to relive my early life. I had not thought of my childhood for years, but it seemed as if God were saying, "You have walked in darkness before, and I brought you out. I will do it again if you will trust me."

PREVIOUS TIMES OF DARKNESS

I had lived through intense darkness as a child. I had also experienced it when I faced death as a teenager in an army uniform. God had brought me through all those times. Why didn't He do it again? I struggled for hope to get me through, one day at a time. I searched for some way out, some answer, some comfort. It wasn't there.

I was still going to sleep at two and three in the morning after walking the floor of the darkened living room, kitchen, and den at night. During the day, I would stumble around, or doze at my desk. Sometimes it was worse. While driving down an open road in my car, the sudden drop of my head would jar me out of a momentary slumber. I would wake up in terror, pinch my leg—to create pain to keep myself awake— and then drive on.

I didn't know it at the time, but after many months of fear, torment, anxiety, and depression, help was on the way. The Word of the Lord was coming with a plan of freedom and deliverance. I could tell this story much faster—I've considered it--but you wouldn't get it. You wouldn't understand. Every one of these words must be written. The ability to hear from God has always led me. So, in reality, this is not a story about one event but the revealing of a brilliant, God-blessed deliverance.

As I've looked back to those difficult times, I realize that all of that time I already had the weapons to defeat the powers of hell in my arsenal. In June of 1951, God had spoken a clear word to me one day while I was driving. I was on a back road between Galveston and Port Arthur, Texas. I had just left an up-lifting conference in Houston, and I was headed to Port Arthur for our Wednesday night service.

I drove down the road rejoicing in my relationship with the Lord. I was singing choruses and old hymns, worshiping God. Suddenly, His manifested presence came into the car, and He said to me, "I am going to put My Word in your mouth, even the word of faith." I didn't know if those words were in the Bible. I had never heard anyone use the phrase "Word of Faith," but I knew God had spoken those exact words. Back in New Orleans, why didn't I speak that powerful word and put a stop to this crazy dilemma? Keep reading, and I will tell you.

CHAPTER 14

What Happened in New Orleans

IN JUNE OF 1953, Barbara and I had no idea of God's plans for us. Nevertheless, in the forty-nine years we pastored, I realize the church defined our lives and molded us in every way—physically, spiritually, and financially. It also shaped our family.

When we started the church in New Orleans, many of the pastors on the radio were preaching against television. One day, a brother went to install carpet in one of the pastors' homes and found a television in the closet of the master bedroom. He got so angry he left the church. You might ask, "How do you know he saw the television and left the church?" That's easy. He became a member of our church and told me the story. Through this, I learned that God has not called us to level harsh judgment but to offer His grace and tell the world of His mercy and love.

THE AIRLINES' QUESTION: "WHERE DO YOU WANT TO GO?"

I sat on the platform one Sunday morning and watched people coming in. God spoke to me these words, "Fifty percent of those people have been divorced; most of them have remarried. What are you going to do with them?" Jesus had an excellent opportunity to judge divorce and remarriage with the woman at the well. He didn't do it. She ran back into the city and declared what she had seen and heard from Jesus. As a result of her words of "evangelism," the people came out, and many believed.

Let's understand: God doesn't like divorce, and neither do I, but it exists. It is not the unpardonable sin. People coming into churches today carry a lot of baggage, so what are we going to do about it? Here is my answer: We should have the same attitude the airlines have. When you walk up to the counter at Delta, American or United Air Lines, they do not inquire where you have been. Instead they ask, "Where do you want to go?"

In the event we allow someone to work with children or young people, we should check him or her out—thoroughly. That's not because we are judgmental but because we are wise. If we become "religious police" and try to whip everyone into shape, we get discouraged when we fail. It is better to teach the Word of God in an encouraging atmosphere, be a joyful example before the world, and let its people see the positive and hopeful product. People will want to be a part of something like that.

THE JEAN SANDERS STORY

Within six months after I arrived in New Orleans, I started a daily radio broadcast. The program lasted for fifteen minutes. I came on the air with a dramatic introduction, expressing who I was, where I was from, the name of my church—Word of Faith Temple—and finally, the name of our broadcast.

I preached Jesus Christ, telling the people what kind of person He was. The Bible says Jesus came "teaching, preaching and healing" (see Matt. 9:35). I spoke of these three things on almost every program. I presented examples of Jesus healing all manner of sicknesses and disease. Then I pointedly explained that He was the same "yesterday, today, and forever." I invited people to send me their prayer requests, promised I would pray for them, and believed Jesus would heal them.

One female listener wrote to me. Her name was Jean Sanders. She had been in the English Air Force, married an American soldier, and ended up living in the United States. She described her situation like this:

I went through the terrible blitz in London. The bombs rained down on us, and I became more frightened every day and especially every night. This went on until it has now destroyed my life. Coming to America has helped a little, but I have received seventeen electrical shock treatments. I have agoraphobia and cannot go outside the house into the crowds around me. I cannot ride on streetcars or any kind of public transportation. I cannot go to grocery stores, clothing stores, or shops of any kind. The doctors believe I will hurt myself and my children if I am left alone with them. My life seemed hopeless until I began to listen to your radio broadcast. I am writing, asking you to help me."

I sat down at my small Royal portable typewriter and answered Jean's letter. First, I prayed for wisdom, asking God to help me articulate the words that would bring hope and healing to her life. I told her about a conference we were beginning soon. I described the services we were to have, and I asked her to come to the church. I told her I was praying she would be able to attend because there was power in the prayers of the whole church coming together in unity.

We started the conference on a Sunday night. I was sitting on the small platform with one of my close preacher friends, Garlon Pemberton. We were ready to start the service when suddenly, I saw a young woman come through the door. Two children walked with her, and she was carrying a younger child in her arms. I quickly told Garlon about her. I knew it was Jean Sanders.

"Garlon, this woman has been writing to me, and I want you to make sure she does not leave until I am able to talk to her."

He agreed. She sat down as the service started. At the end, I gave a salvation invitation, telling the people we would not only lead them to Jesus but we would also pray for all of those who had physical or emotional needs.

Jean walked down the aisle and knelt at our wooden altar. My sweet mother-in-law held her children and assured her they would be well-tended. I went and spoke to Jean, making sure of her identity. I led her to the Lord and called for the other ministers to join me in praying for her. Suddenly, the Spirit and power of God came upon her. She began to weep and then to laugh for joy.

Jean kept a journal. Later, her daughter Marie sent me a copy of the page she wrote the next day. She had drawn a pencil picture of Jesus on the page and written these words:

I drew this picture the day I went to the Word of Faith Temple for the first time. Took my 3 babies. The Lord worked wonders for me. MY HEART IS HIS. I AM HIS. He gave me his Peace. I have found Jesus... Today was MY DAY.

The date was at the bottom of the page—1st July 54.

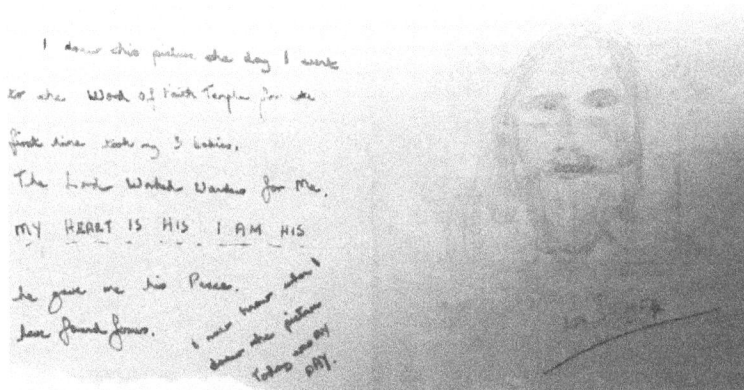

That night, Jean was instantly and totally delivered. She could leave her home, go to any store, and ride any public transportation. A few weeks later, Mardi Gras came to New Orleans with its vast crowds. She took gospel tracts from our church and walked through the streets, giving them to everyone she met. She became one of the greatest soul-winners in our church. She also became a close friend to Barbara and me.

Years later, we were with her on the night she died. She lay on her bed, laughing and crying for joy. Looking at us, she said, "I can see heaven coming to me. Jesus is waiting for me!" We went into the living room and waited with the family. Suddenly, there came a sound from her bedroom like the wings of a great eagle flying away. We rushed into her room. Jean had finally completed her journey. She was home—with Jesus.

CHAPTER 15

"The Word of the Lord Came"

EVEN AFTER SENDING MY sister, Jean Sanders, home to be with the Lord, the heaviness of my spirit did not lift. Something had to change. I was drained by the struggle. I was weary of the games I was playing before the church, acting as if everything were fine while living in suffocating fear. I had not stopped praying. I still preached. I still pastored the church. My marriage was still intact. I still loved my children, and I still loved God. But the "feelings" part of myself was miserable.

I found that at times I could be very wise and, in a godly manner, counsel others and help them find forgiveness. I couldn't, however, heal myself. I thought I knew how, but when the pressure was on, I just remembered the phrase from the musical *Annie*, "It's a hard knock life," and I believed I would have to learn to live with it. This, though, is the big lie, and God was about to give me just a glimpse of that.

I was trying so hard to grow in my faith and be perfect, but it was hopeless, and I felt it. One day in my office, the Bible was open, and somehow, I saw Paul's words staring up at me:

But we have this treasure in earthen vessels, that the excellency of the power may be of God, and not of us. We are troubled on every side [pushed around], yet not distressed; we are perplexed, but not in despair; Persecuted, but not forsaken; cast down, but not destroyed . . . For which cause we faint not; but though our outward man perish, *yet the inward man is renewed day by day* (2 Cor.4:7-9, 16, emphasis mine).

Many times I had read Paul's words, but that time, I began to speak my own words to God. "Lord God, I am troubled on every side. I am perplexed. I am persecuted. I am cast down!" But then I finished the whole thought. When I did this, I felt the healing balm of God's loving presence, and suddenly my audible words changed in tone and content. "O God, I *do* have a great treasure in my life. I *don't* have to do it alone. The excellency of the power is from God and *not* my human ability. I am *not* forsaken, God loves me, and the overwhelming majority of God's people love and appreciate me."

Then I got to the part where Paul said, "The inward man is being renewed day by day." I instantly cried out, "O God, please renew me." It was then I understood that I had been running on an empty tank, and I was disheartened.

I had to let God fill up my tank—even when I had done nothing to deserve it—and let others show their gratitude and supply my emotional needs. I became even more excited. My source of supply was abundant! It took a little while, but I became more patient and began to let others pour on the healing oil and wine. There were days when nothing happened, but when I waited on Him, God would initiate renewing my spirit. I began to open my heart to the people, and they filled my life with good things, things that would crowd out the old depression, fears, and torment.

Apart from complete renewal, which I continued to wait for, I was destined to stumble around and play church. I was compelled to put on a false "preacher face" but never be transformed. I realize now that God was using His Word to slowly bring change to me. That was not all, however, He was also using songs, worship, and praise. Someone brought a chorus to our church that I had not heard before, and I walk the floor many nights singing the words over and over:

From glory to glory He's changing me, changing me,
*   changing me,*
His likeness and image to perfect in me—
The love of God shown to the world.
He's changing, changing me, from earthly things to
*   the heavenly,*
His likeness and image to perfect in me—

The love of God shown to the world.

—"From Glory to Glory," author unknown

THE WORD OF THE LORD CAME

Over one hundred times in the Bible, we read this statement: "The word of the Lord came . . ." Sometimes, "the
word of the Lord came to Elijah," at other times to Jeremiah
or another of the Old Testament prophets. I heard my Word
from the Lord while I was driving on Interstate 10 toward
New Orleans. I had crossed a high bridge over the Industrial
Waterway that runs from Corpus Christi, Texas, through
New Orleans, Louisiana, to Tampa, Florida. As I passed over
the apex of the bridge, I hit the steering wheel and cried out
to an empty car, but really to God, "How long am I going to
have to put up with this awful dread—this torment?"

I paused to catch my breath, and suddenly I heard these
words: "Your deliverance is in My Word."

It sounded so simple. I knew the power of the Bible—the
Word of God. I had been reading the Bible all through these
difficult months, and I had received temporary help. And, I
emphasize temporary. All through the rest of that day, the
Word wouldn't leave my mind. When the Word of God came
to me, the wisdom of God came also. The Lord laid out His
plan in no uncertain terms. God told me exactly what to do,
and I determined to put the plan into operation immediately. The next day, I gathered the materials I needed to carry
out the plan.

Before I left my office, I collected the following five things and took them home with me: a large Bible with thicker paper so the pages would be easier to turn and write on; *Strong's Exhaustive Concordance* so I could find the location of any word in the Bible; *Webster's Fifth Edition Collegiate Dictionary,* my college dictionary; *Roget's Thesaurus*; and a new yellow legal pad.

That night after our evening meal, I spread all these things across the table. It was time to go to work. My first objective was to think of every word that could possibly relate to the way I was feeling: anxiety, frustration, fear, dread, trepidation, foreboding, torment, downheartedness, misery, melancholy, depression, terror, despair, and the list goes on. I took each word and looked it up in the dictionary, then in the thesaurus, searching for synonyms and all possible descriptions. When I finished, I had over a dozen listed on my legal pad.

The most poignant word to me was *fear.* So I put *fear* at the top of the next page. I then took the *Strong's Concordance* and looked up every place it occurred in the Bible—beginning in Genesis and all the way through Revelation. My objective was to find exactly what the Word of God had to say about it. I was especially looking for God's promises in dealing with fear.

I wrote only the scriptural reference in the left margin of my yellow legal pad. When I finished the first word, I had many pages filled. This took hours. (*Fear* and other forms of the word appear about 500 times in *Strong's Concordance.*) I then put the next word at the top of a new page and started the whole process again. When I finished with all the words, I had pages and pages—from the top of the page to the bottom—of nothing but Bible references in the left margins. Then, I pushed the dictionary, thesaurus, and concordance aside. Only the Bible and the many pages I had filled in my yellow legal pad remained.

I am glad there were no computers in those days. You can use one, but there was just something about my fingers running over the pages of the Bible that touched my soul. I started in Genesis and read each verse, asking these questions: Is this only a history, a special passage, or a promise for another age or time? Is this verse, this promise, only for one person or group of persons? Could it be for me?

If I felt it applied to me, I defined it so that the message or promise fit on one line of the legal pad. I would read it over and over, often putting my name into the verse. I especially enjoyed doing this when I came to Psalm 91.

He that dwells in the secret place of the most High shall abide under the shadow of the Almighty. I will say of the Lord, He is *Charles Green's* refuge and fortress: his God; in him *Charles Green* will trust. Surely, he shall deliver *Charles Green* from the snare of the fowler... *Charles Green* shall not be afraid for the terror by night... nor for the pestilence that walks in darkness... There shall no evil befall *Charles Green*, neither shall any plague come nigh his dwelling. *Charles Green* shall call upon me, and I will answer him: I will be with him in trouble; I will deliver *Charles Green,* and honor him. With long life will I satisfy *Charles Green,* and show him my salvation.

CHAPTER 16

Deliverance Came One Night

EACH NIGHT, I FOLLOWED this routine unceasingly from the time the children and Barbara went to bed until I could keep my eyes open no longer. Then came that singular and never-to-be-forgotten night. Everyone had gone to bed earlier than usual, and I had been reading verse after verse, promise after promise for over an hour. Suddenly, I read one verse that electrified me. The words seemed to jump out of the page into my life. I put my finger on the location of the verse, and I said aloud—not in my mind but with my voice, "God, that promise is for me. I'm going to stand on that Word."

And then I began to laugh, and I said, "I'm really going to do it. I'm going to stand on the Word." I took off my slippers, I spread the Bible on the floor, and I planted both of my feet on the two opened pages. I stood there for many minutes, thanking and praising God for His Word and confessing my faith in that Word. The powerful presence of God became so real, I could hardly stand.

I usually sat at the table reading and working until one or two in the morning. But that night, something different happened. I must have picked the Bible up off the floor—I remember picking up the Bible, but I don't remember anything from the ensuing hour. I must have placed it back on the table, but I don't remember putting the Bible on the table. I don't remember sitting down. I don't remember anything. I lost consciousness!

I awakened about an hour later with my arms on the table and my head on the Bible. Slowly I arose and pushed the Bible away from the edge. Then I walked out of the kitchen-dinette room, turning off the light as I passed the switch. Entering the bedroom, I was so sleepy that I dropped my robe on the floor. I remember slipping into the bed, and I was gone! I woke up at seven in the morning. I had slept almost an hour on the table; I then spent seven hours in bed—asleep. That had not happened for seven months. No pain pills. No sleep medication. Nothing—but God!

The most striking thing I remember about waking up that morning is this: The fog was gone from my brain, and the feeling of foreboding and unease had vanished. I was free! I knew I was free. And I knew how it had happened. I had sat at the table, night after night, filling my mind and my life with the powerful words of God. I had not only read those words; I had read them aloud. And that spoken Word had slowly but surely worked within me until it had produced the answer, my deliverance.

PEOPLE HAVE QUESTIONS

What had caused all my problems? I'm positive I know the answer to that question now, but before I give you that information, I need to answer a few other questions I am often asked. People wonder what singular verse could have been so powerful that it broke those oppressive bonds and freed me. Here's the problem: I don't remember the verse. For the life of me, I cannot remember the particular passage that captured my heart and produced instantaneous deliverance. And, much to everyone else's chagrin, I'm glad I don't.

My deliverance did not come because I had discovered a secret formula. And it wasn't just what I had done that night. For more than two weeks, I had actively searched for a biblical solution. That had led to my walking through the Word of God—in faith! As never before in my life, I had immersed myself in the Word. Most importantly—I believe—I verbally confessed the Word of God from the pages of the Bible, and the Word of God in my mouth created fresh hope and fresh faith in. In addition, God's grace as I faithfully continued in prayer, Bible study, and preaching the Word—regardless of how I felt—set the stage for that one night's dramatic deliverance.

Another question I am frequently asked is, "Does the oppression ever try to come back on you again?" My answer is unequivocally, "Yes." But now it's different. I know the road to freedom. I know the power of the spoken Word of God. The audible Word of God can overpower the torment of the mind. This is why it's important to memorize the Word of God. The devil hates God, and he hates God's Word. In any contest with the devil, quote the Word of God to Him.

JESUS QUOTED THE WORD OF GOD TO THE DEVIL

It's what Jesus did when He was led by the Spirit of God into the wilderness. When Satan came to Him, Jesus could have said words like these: "You can't hurt me. You can't defeat or overcome me. You know why? I'm the Son of God. I am omnipotent—all-powerful. I am omniscient—all-knowing. I am omnipresent—I inhabit the universe. I am eternal—I had no beginning, and I'll have no ending."

If that is what He had said, we would not be able to relate to His words. So, He did not speak words about Himself. Instead, He quoted Scripture. Let's see what Jesus really did say. It will help you win victory instead of walk in defeat. Jesus' words will give you the solid foundation upon which I learned to walk to secure my deliverance. What worked for me will certainly work for you!

CHAPTER 17

From Condemnation to Victory

So, what had caused all my problems? I believe those seven months of torment came mainly because of two things: my work ethic and my past teachings that brought condemnation into my life and ministry. Both existed because of my background. First, I'd watched many preachers as I grew up. I was fortunate to have four great men of God as my pastors: D. F. "Frank" Warren, W. H. "Bill" Marshall, M. H. "Marvin" Hansford, and W. H. "Bill" McCann. They all loved God and joyfully sacrificed for His work.

Unfortunately, I'd also come into contact with others who were different. Some spent more time fishing, playing golf, or sleeping than working for the ministry. None of these activities are sinful, but when men put them first, they become sin. Other ministers I had known were just lazy and took their callings for granted.

I decided I would be a hard worker for God and the church, working 24/7 to redeem the ministry. When we started the church in New Orleans, I worked at it seven days a week, all day and into every night. If someone called me at four in the morning, I hesitated to say I had been sleeping. I wanted to be awake for every call, answer every request, fulfill every expectation, finish every assignment, and solve everyone problem. Trying to do all five of those things almost killed me.

Monday through Friday, I worked in my office, pastored the church, performed six radio broadcasts, and practically lived in hospitals as I visited the sick. If anyone called and asked me to go, I went. I did my studying for ministry at night when I got home. I filled my Saturdays with counseling sessions because people would call, saying, "I can only come on Saturday."

I taught Sunday school on Sunday morning, preached Sunday morning, Sunday night, and Wednesday night, and led a Bible study on Thursday morning. Each of these required hours of preparation. I had no outside recreation. I did not hunt, fish, or play golf. I took no part in sports activities. I worked and lived with the feeling that I was not doing enough.

In counseling sessions, people presented me with lists of impossible circumstances and then ask me, "What am

I going to do?" I would go home and lie awake, trying to find answers for them. I was compelled to do it. I was the pastor. But in all these things, I never felt I was doing enough.

And, the condemnation was suffocating. Even though I knew the theological difference between works and grace, I acted as if grace were for everyone else; I had to do the work. I did not realize it at the time, but I could not enjoy a day off and was never comfortable when on vacations. I always took work with me. I hate to think of what would have happened if I had owned a cell phone.

AFTER MY DELIVERANCE, EVERYTHING CHANGED

I still remember with great delight the first time a person gave me his list of all those impossible circumstances. "I can't do this, and I can't do that—so tell me, Pastor; what am I going to do?" I looked straight into the eyes of that person, paused for a moment, and then answered the question with a question. "I don't know—what *are* you going to do?" For me, that was a victory.

I started an exercise program. I tried to jog around a track at the YMCA and could only manage a quarter of a mile. In eleven months, I had lost forty pounds, and I was running three miles at a good pace.

Barbara and I also took a vacation to Hawaii. When she saw how I loved the place and the people, she was glad I was having a great time. But when she saw me go for one week and never call home to make sure the church was doing well, she knew her husband had been rescued from himself.

WHY DID IT HAPPEN?

I close this chapter with a warning. It is not enough to get help and win some victories. It is important that we learn how to keep secure that which we have won. It is true that I won a great victory, and all credit must go to God. But there is one more question I am often asked: "Why? Why did it happen?" There could be many reasons.

Perhaps I developed some kind of chemical imbalance in my body, but I doubt it.

Perhaps a multitude of demonic spirits from some distant shore decided to attack me, destroy my life and home, and wreck our church. I doubt this too. It's possible, but I don't think that is what happened to me. Don't misunderstand me. I do believe satanic activity was involved. I believe all fear, all torment, all anxiety, all depression, all sickness, and all disease are ultimately satanic in origin.

From the moment of Adam's transgression and rebellion against God, the perfect world and God's perfect people were gone. Sin had come, sickness had come, and death had come into the world. Starting from that moment, we see human beings struggling with their lives, relationships, problems, and temptations—essentially, struggling with the reality of sin.

My problem was not caused by an act of sin; nevertheless, all problems come as the result of sin's presence in the world.

Our present problems ("Why would a good God allow bad things to happen?") all began with Adam's transgression. The word "sorrow" was first mentioned to Eve in the garden. The word "sweat" came into existence when God told Adam he would make his living by the "sweat of your face." Before that, God made the plants, the trees, and the fruit to grow, and man's responsibility was only to "dress it and keep it" (Gen. 2:15).

CHAPTER 18

The Truth About My Four Big Fears

MY FOUR MAJOR FEARS never materialized, but the possibility that they would almost destroyed me. Considering events that happened in the decade following my release, they seem light and momentary in comparison.

My first fear—I'm afraid about our church: When God delivered me, everything began to change. The church sprang forth into new life. Our crowds increased; long-time members and attenders developed new enthusiasm. That fear that our church was going to fail was caused by a lie! When I looked at things differently, they indeed became different.

When my faith returned, and when I acted in harmony with it, the church responded in a miraculous way.

Before Hurricane Katrina hit New Orleans and the Gulf Coast in August 2005, our church was located on a thirty-eight-acre campus with a quarter-mile frontage on Interstate 10. Thousands of people were being blessed—not only in New Orleans but also in southern Louisiana, Mississippi, and around the world. Great buildings housed our congregation. Our K-12 school had operated for thirty-one years and then it all screeched to a halt with Katrina's destruction of millions of dollars of property. When Barbara and I retired, due to God's faithfulness, the church did not even have to worry about mortgage payments. We were totally debt free with $600,000 in our cash account.

My second fear—I'm afraid I can't take care of my family: This also proved to be a lie. God has supplied all our needs, and most of the time, even our wants. Since I came to New Orleans in June of 1953, every debt has been paid. Not one bill was ever overdue with our family or the church. We lived in seven different houses, each one better than the one before. Our children did not suffer financially because of the ministry; rather, they were blessed in many, many ways. Because of the ministry, they traveled to exciting places all over America. They own their own homes, drive their own cars, and enjoy God's blessings. They have also live lives of faith.

My third fear—I'm afraid something bad is going to happen to one of my children: I did not grow up around children. I was reared alone. When my children were born, I loved them and treasured them greatly. Whatever we had to do to take care of them was not a sacrifice but a constant delight. We tried to shield them from the pressure we often experienced. I now look back and see some of my failures as a parent. I have wished I could try it again and do a better job. That is probably true in every facet of my life, but I don't dwell on it anymore. What's done is done.

Many nights during my ordeal, I would lie in the bed and visualize my children being crushed under car wheels. At other times, I would see someone drag their lifeless bodies out of the water. These visions are why I would give Barbara detailed instructions before I left the house: Don't let anyone take the children anywhere in a car. Don't let them go to the swimming pool with anyone. (I made sure they both became excellent swimmers.) My words became a heavy burden for Barbara to bear.

However, even in my torment, I did not let the devil win the battle. One day, when the torment about my children became too strong for me, I drove my car to the lakefront of Lake Pontchartrain. I got out of the car, walked over to the seawall, sat down, and did a strange thing. I visualized the funerals of my two children; I watched their bodies being rolled down the aisle of the church, and I saw myself walking to the pulpit to speak at their funerals. At the end of this imaginary scene, I began to talk out loud to the devil:

"I don't believe this will ever happen. I believe it is a lie sent to torment me. But if it should ever happen, I declare this to you and before God: The next Sunday morning, my heart will be broken, but I will stand in the pulpit; I will stand before the world and preach the gospel. Devil, you are a liar, the father of lies, and you don't have the ability to tell the truth! I will not quit." After that, I got up, walked to my car, and drove away. That part of my fear left and never returned. I was beginning to win.

Through the years, we all—Barbara, Michael, Cynthia, and I—have had some physical problems. God has delivered us from every one of them. Today, we have minor problems of one kind or another, but we have been blessed of God.

My son, Michael, and his wife, Linda, have two boys—Geoffrey and Tyler, and the blessings of God have been extended to our grandchildren. Cyndy and her husband, Matt, live in a beautiful home in Texas and enjoy a great life with each other—and God.

My fourth fear—I am not afraid of death, but I *am* afraid I am going to die and leave my family alone: Until I was delivered, every minor physical problem became a major concern. I had worried especially about the knot on my right side, fearing it was the beginning of a cancer that would kill me. On that wonderful night, God took that fear away. Over fifty years have passed. I did not die. I have not died. I am still alive. The knot is still there, and it's become a joke in our family. Many times, when Cynthia was younger and not getting her way, she would playfully raise her fist and threaten, "I'm going to hit your knot." That remark has always brought a good laugh.

I'M GLAD IT HAPPENED

I am now going to make a statement that will probably shock you. At the time, I never dreamed I could come to the time and place that I could make this statement, but here it is: "I am glad this thing happened to me!" Was I glad at the time? Of course not! I was suffering. I was hurting. And I was not a fool. But now, things are different. Now, I am on the other side. I **was** on the hurting, fearful, tormented side. Now, I am on the *victory side!*

What was happening to me seemed horrible at the time. Now I realize it led to great victory. It totally changed me as a person, and it changed my perspective on ministry. Before this time, I struggled because I imagined conflict with many people in the church. There was absolutely no evidence to back it up, but the devil would lie to me, "They are waiting to find some fault in you that will hurt you and the church." The Bible says he is a liar, and the truth is not in him. I had learned this—the hard way.

In victory, I began to walk with confidence in God and His Word. I began to rejoice every day in his blessings, His favor and His presence. I could feel them in my life and ministry.

Before this experience, we had scores of people in our church. By the time I retired from the Word of Faith congregation, we had thousands. Without this battle, without the great victory God gave, it never would have happened. That is what Andrae Crouch was saying in his song "Through It All."

I thank God for the mountains, and I thank Him for
*   the valleys;*
I thank Him for the storms He brought me through.
For if I'd never had a problem, I wouldn't know God could
*   solve them;*
I'd never know what faith in God could do.
And the chorus of that wonderful song says the same
*   thing I have been sharing with you about my*
*   own struggles:*
Through it all,
Through it all, I've learned to trust in Jesus,
I've learned to trust in God.
Through it all,
Through it all, I've learned to depend upon His Word.

When my time of victory came, it came because I learned to depend on the Word of God. I ended up "standing on the Word of God"—literally.

WHAT ABOUT YOU?

It is good for you to know God came to my rescue, but it is more important for you to know God wants to rescue you. He wants to bless you. He wants to give you great favor. God wants to give you faith, power, and miracles that will cause your enemy to be defeated.

It is time for you to declare the Word of God against your enemy the devil and all his co-workers. And you don't have to rely on paper to do this. If I were seeking help from God's Word today, here is what I would do: I would take the words "fear" and "depression" and run them through the computer Bible. When I had found the words I thought would apply to my problem, I would copy them and print them on a created document.

When I had all the words printed, I would push everything aside and go to a place where I could read them aloud, seeing the words with my own eyeballs and hearing my own voice speaking the words of God. I would do this over and over through many days and nights. I would absolutely forget television and every other distraction. I'd read no other books—only the Bible and the special passages.

As the Word grows in you, it will bring forth a response from you. Your first reaction should be faith in the Word. The next is obedience to the Word. Somewhere along the way, this Word will explode within you—and through the Word and the power of the Holy Spirit, your healing and deliverance will come!

Here in the Amplified Bible are the beautiful and powerful words of Isaiah 54:17:

But no weapon that is formed against you shall prosper, and every tongue that shall rise against you in judgment you shall show to be in the wrong. This [peace, righteousness, security, triumph over opposition] is the heritage of the servants of the Lord [those in whom the ideal Servant of the Lord is reproduced]; this is the righteousness or the vindication which they obtain from Me [this is that which I impart to them as their justification], says the Lord.

If you will be faithful amidst trials, tribulations, and tests, God will vindicate your stand. My testimony is very clear: Through the times of darkness in my life, God has been faithful to me, and I have gained in my ability to be more faithful to Him.

My ministry has changed since those difficult days too. I had studied a lot of theology, but no one had ever taught me how to use the Word of God like a weapon of warfare. I am surrounded by minister friends who walk in faith and speak the Word of Faith. I have learned the value of godly relationships in fighting any satanic battle. Today, I would just pick up the phone.

SOME PERSONAL ADVICE

1. Learn to use the Word of God as a mighty weapon of warfare.
2. Surround yourself with godly and spiritually powerful friends, then trust them.

3. Stay faithful to God, resting in His promises and believing better days are coming.

"Let us hold fast the profession of our faith without wavering; (for he is faithful that promised)" (Heb. 10:23), and "All of the promises of God begin and are fulfilled in Jesus" (2 Cor. 1:20).

SECTION V: **A PASTOR'S WISDOM**

CHAPTER 19

How Jesus Handled Temptations and Spiritual Warfare

THREE TIMES THE DEVIL came with his words of temptation, and each time Jesus used the same power. He used what I call "Word Power."

Then was Jesus led up of the Spirit into the wilderness to be tempted of the devil.

And when he had fasted forty days and forty nights, he was afterward an hungered.

And when the tempter came to him, he said, If thou be the Son of God, command that these stones be made bread.

But he answered and said, *It is written*, Man shall not live by bread alone, but by every word that proceedeth out of the mouth of God (Matt. 4:1-4, emphasis mine).

In dealing with our abundant supply (whether it be bread or other things), we need to remember what Jesus said. "It is written!" We live and walk in victory by learning what God says on any subject and then speaking that same conclusive word.

Then the devil taketh him up into the holy city, and setteth him on a pinnacle of the temple, And saith unto him, If thou be the Son of God, cast thyself down: for *it is written,* He shall give his angels charge concerning thee: and in their hands they shall bear thee up, lest at any time thou dash thy foot against a stone.

Jesus said unto him, *It is written* again, Thou shalt not tempt the Lord thy God (Matt. 4:5-7, emphasis mine).

We should not tempt God by flying a small airplane without functioning instruments in a thunderstorm. We should not tempt God by going to a fortune-teller or playing any other kind of foolish game of chance. We learn the will of God for our lives by prayer, reading the Word of God, and walking in the knowledge of the Holy Spirit. We also follow the pattern of those who have a proven ministry in the Kingdom of God. We must learn to discern the voice of God in our personal lives.

Again, the devil taketh him up into an exceeding high mountain, and sheweth him all the kingdoms of the world, and the glory of them; And saith unto him, All these things will I give thee, if thou wilt fall down and worship me. Then saith Jesus unto him, Get thee hence, Satan: for *it is written*, Thou shalt worship the Lord thy God, and him only shalt thou serve. Then the devil leaveth him, and, behold, angels came and ministered unto him (Matt. 4:8-11, emphasis mine).

I have heard people say, "I just worship my children. I love them so much." I would not make that statement. I love my wife, and I love my children and grandchildren, but I do not worship them. I worship God. I worship Jesus. Period.

I also appreciate every good thing God has ever put in my life. But that appreciation is nothing compared to the love I have for the Lord Jesus Christ and His Kingdom. I enjoy people and belongings, but if I don't have them tomorrow, I will still love God, rejoice in His presence, and thank Him for His love and salvation.

The apostle Paul had the right idea:

Not that I speak in respect of want: for I have learned, in whatever state I am, therewith to be content. I know both how to be abased [to be low, have little], and I know how to abound [to be high, have plenty]: everywhere and in all things, I am instructed both to be full and to be hungry, both to abound and to suffer need. I can do all things through Christ who strengthens me (Phil. 4:11-13).

I have known people to go into depression when they lose some of their "things." In Hurricane Katrina, Barbara and I lost almost everything we owned, and it was six months before we knew whether the insurance company would pay--let alone how much. However, by God's grace, we never lived in frustration or distress for even one day.

JESUS, THE POWERFUL WORD-MAN

In the beginning was the Word, and the Word was with God, and the Word was God. The same was in the beginning with God. All things were made by him; and without him was not any thing made that was made... And the Word was made flesh, and dwelt among us, (and we beheld his glory, the glory as of the only begotten of the Father), full of grace and truth (John 1:1-3, 14).

He is talking about the Word that was "with" God and "was" God. This is the same Jesus who was tempted by the devil. There is no doubt, Jesus is God in the flesh, but in all three temptations, in all three satanic attacks, Jesus never once used "God Power." Instead, each time, He used "Word Power!" *It is written.*

We have the same power. We have the written Word of God, and when we speak it, it becomes the spoken Word of God.

When I fill my mind with God's Word, *I think like God.*

When I fill my mouth with God's Word, *I talk like God.*

When I believe the written Word and act on the spoken Word—my faith confession—I win my victories as Jesus won His.

When torment comes against you, speak the Word of God aloud. Your voice, speaking God's Word, will overpower your mind when it tries to dwell on negative, ungodly, tormenting thoughts. Here in the book of Romans, God is showing the close relationship between believing with one's heart and confessing with one's mouth. If we really believe it, we must *say* it.

[The righteousness which is by faith says] The word is nigh thee, even in thy mouth, and in thy heart: that is, the word of faith, which we preach; That if thou shalt confess with thy mouth the Lord Jesus, and shalt believe in thine heart that God hath raised him from the dead, thou shalt be saved. For with the heart man believeth unto righteousness; and with the mouth confession is made unto salvation. For the scripture saith, Whosoever believeth on him shall not be ashamed. For there is no difference between the Jew and the Greek: for the same Lord over all is rich unto all that call upon him. For whosoever shall call upon the name of the Lord shall be saved [Greek: sozo, salvation, healing, and deliverance] (Rom. 10:8-13).

CHAPTER 20

The Secret of the Little Light

A s children of God, walking in the anointing of the Holy Spirit, we can expect to be led by our Father God through the Holy Spirit Who dwells in us. Romans 8:14 tells us this: "For as many as are led by the Spirit of God, they are the sons of God."

As I have written this story, I'm still amazed that—after all the wonderful things God had done in me, through me, and for me—I could stand by the bedroom window and feel fear and terror because a little light bulb was not burning on a pole across the street.

Looking out of the bedroom window and gazing at that little light brought comfort. It sounds foolish, except for one thing. I now know the secret of the little light. In the darkness of my emotions, I was yearning for light. In my life and in my travels around the world, I've seen the competition between the dark and the light. The natural world is filled with glitter, and we Christians are often dull.

The world has learned the secret of light in advertising its companies and products, and although I have been in New York City many times, I am still fascinated by Broadway. No wonder they call it "The Great White Way." When I am in Tokyo, I always go to see the lights of the Ginza. These two lighted ways draw millions of people every year. The astronaut crews can easily see the lights of Broadway and the Ginza from outer space. There is something about light that pulls us in.

Millions of children sit with little boxes in their hands, their thumbs frantically pressing little buttons while lights dance in front of them. Sometimes they are in the boxing ring, defeating the world heavyweight champion. Sometimes they are racing their cars around the tracks. At other times, they are involved in a deadly karate match. And it is all done with light.

When our troops went to the Gulf War in Iraq, our pilots were more than prepared for tactical mancuvers. One article I read told the reason. Little boys and girls, holding Game Boys or the controllers for Play Stations and Game Cubes had learned to quickly respond to the lighted figures that jumped on the screens. Now, they were instantly responding to the controls on their planes and to the tactics of the enemies that were coming against them. And I read a medical article in our local newspaper saying that surgeons entering practice today are the best in the history of the world, and it gave the same reason—rapid thumbs and fingers working on their tiny "light boxes" have prepared them for delicate surgical techniques.

And of course, we cannot forget the "light box" that is not only in every home but in almost every room of our homes. It is the light miracle of the millennium: television. Moving out of the analog world into digital technology, commercial messages can now make flashlight batteries, floor wax, bug spray, and baking powder look exciting. And it's all done with light. Once we had to use Western Union Telegraph to send messages. Now, we text, practically at the speed of light

THE LIGHT OVER ISRAEL

God surely showed off His "Light Power" to the children of Israel. As this bunch of slaves came out of their Egyptian bondage, God wanted them to see who was now in charge. He brought them through the Red Sea, the walls of water piling up on either side while they walked through on dry ground. On the other side, God placed a pillar of cloud by day and fire by night (Ex. 13:21).

This fire-light cloud probably served many purposes. It gave them warmth during the cool Sinai nights, protected them from the heat during the days, and warned their enemies: no trespassing! God wanted His light to be the comforting power of His holy presence. And when the cloud moved, they moved. They did not need a map. The light-cloud led the way.

THE LITTLE RED TRAIN

There is no doubt about it; we are attracted to light. I was attending a basketball game, watching the New Orleans Pelicans play in their beautiful arena. We were about ten minutes in, and my son, Michael, slapped me on the shoulder.

"Hey, did you see that layup?"

"No, I didn't see it."

"I thought you were watching this game!"

"No, I have been watching the little train."

About eighteen or twenty feet above the court, there was an "advertising channel" traveling around and around the elliptical arena. My eyes had been drawn to the moving lights of a little red train. The sports organization had paid hundreds of millions of dollars to put the team on the court. It probably cost them a few hundred dollars every night to put up the advertisement with the little red train. And I was watching the train instead of the game. That is the power of light! If we will light up what we are doing—our businesses, our churches, our sermons, our colleges, and our products—people will be drawn to us and our message.

Growing up, I was often bored with church. When I finally knew I was going to be preaching the Word of God, and we opened our first church, I decided it was not going to be boring and dull. We always lit up everything around us in New Orleans. When we laid our first cornerstone, I did not want boring statistics listed on it. I did not want it to have my name, the names of the building committee members, the year we started, or the year of some other special occasion. So here's the phrase we did use: "Dedicated to the Exaltation of the Lord Jesus Christ and the Proclamation of His Kingdom."

These words—*exaltation, Lord Jesus Christ, proclamation,* and *kingdom*—are exciting. They shine. And for over fifty years, our church has shined with all colors, races, and denominations of desperate people leaving their troubled lives behind and coming home to God.

I hope many pastors will read this book and be encouraged. Let me share this word with you. What we have may be *theological, spiritual,* and even *religious,* but people will not come to our location and "buy" into the message if our meetings are dull, dark, and boring. If we don't shine—forget it! Our listeners will feel bereft, and they'll be left yearning for the Light.

CHAPTER 21

Valuable Examples

JOSEPH WAS ONE OF my constant companions during my months of agony. I read the story of Joseph over and over. I felt like changing my name to "Joseph." From the first moment I read his story, I identified with him. Growing up, I suffered frequent hurts. In many situations I felt rejected, and I would go to my Bible storybook, once again reading about Joseph. His story has brought me great comfort and reassurance my whole life.

JOSEPH—GOD'S PROMISE FULFILLED

Joseph had everything going for him. He had a good home, and his father loved him. But then a problem developed. Perhaps I should say his problems began when God gave him a dream. His brothers did not like the interpretation of the dream, and they plotted against him.

"And Joseph dreamed a dream, and he told it his brethren: and they hated him yet the more" (Gen. 37:5).

They put him in a pit and took the blood of an animal and showed it to their father, telling him it was Joseph's blood and that his son was dead. Some Midianite merchantmen came by, and the brothers sold Joseph to those Ishmaelites for twenty pieces of silver. They took Joseph to Egypt and sold him to a military man by the name of Potiphar (Gen. 37:28). Joseph ended up in prison after a false accusation by Potiphar's wife. Many people treated him unjustly, but God was with him and showed mercy to him.

Ultimately, Joseph was brought before Pharaoh, who had experienced a disturbing dream. He told Pharaoh what the dream was and then gave Pharaoh the correct interpretation. For this, Joseph received a reward. He became the second ruler in all of Egypt. The Bible tells of this encounter in such a powerful way in Psalm 105:17-22 (emphasis mine):

He [God] sent a man before them, even Joseph, who was sold for a servant: Whose feet they hurt with fetters: he was laid in iron: *Until the time that his word came*: the word of the Lord tried him. The king [Pharaoh], the ruler of the people let him go free. He made him lord of his house, and ruler over all his substance To bind princes at his pleasure, and teach his senators wisdom. Joseph had the authority to arrest the other princes, using only the authority of His own word. He was so wise, he taught Pharaoh's senators wisdom.

The fact that we go through trials in our lives does not mean God does not love us. Even though we get mistreated, it does not mean God is trying to kill us or is angry with us. It does not mean God is unfair. It does not mean He has abandoned us.

When Joseph's brothers came to Egypt seeking food, they came to this great assistant ruler in Egypt, falling before him in submission. It must have been a great shock when the "ruler" was revealed to be their brother Joseph:

And his brethren also went and fell down before his face; and they said, Behold, we be thy servants. And Joseph said unto them, Fear not: for am I in the place of God?

But as for you, ye thought evil against me; but God meant it unto good, to bring to pass, as it is this day, to save much people alive (Gen. 50:18-50, emphasis mine).

Our good God allowed all of this to happen not only to save Joseph and his family but also to save many Egyptians. In Genesis 12:3, God said He would bless all the families of the earth through Abraham. We neither see this happening during Abraham's life nor with Isaac's or Jacob's. We do not see this happening until Joseph comes into the picture. Then the heathen Egyptians began to feel the results of God's love, mercy, grace, and forgiveness.

JESUS—THE BEST PICTURE GOD EVER TOOK

In one of E. Stanley Jones' small books, he told the story of a little boy in Sunday school. The teacher asked the class, "Does anyone know who Jesus was?" The little fellow raised his hand and said, "He was the best picture God ever took."

Jesus came to reveal this good God and demonstrate His good works. When the apostle Peter came to the house of Cornelius, his assignment was to introduce Jesus to the Gentiles. He did so by telling them, "God anointed Jesus of Nazareth with the Holy Ghost and with power: *who went about doing good*, and healing all that were oppressed of the devil; for God was with him" (Acts 10:38, emphasis mine). Jesus did not go about acting religious. He went about doing good.

People were drawn to both of these men because of their servant attitudes, and the same thing should be happening to us. Like Joseph and like Jesus, the greatest path of deliverance from our own anxieties and depressions comes when we are wrapped up in God's plans for our unselfish service to others.

CHAPTER 22

From Light to Life

I N THE NEW TESTAMENT, we have another illustration in Peter. Divinely called and then "Jesus-trained," he goes out and heals the sick and announces the Kingdom of God. However, he soon comes under pressure. Jesus is headed for the cross, and Peter is standing away from Him, cursing and denying the Lord, even saying, "I don't know the man!"

The scene changes again, and in fifty days, he is standing before the people of Israel, thundering with great power, calling them to repentance and faith in Jesus, the Christ. What has happened? Certainly not the mere discussion of "Jesus theology." Certainly not the shaming and pressure from the other disciples to shape up.

The answer is simple: Peter saw the light. He received a special invitation from the resurrected Lord, the One who said, "I am the light of the world" (John 8:12b, 9:5b). He saw the nail prints on the hands of Jesus and the spear mark in His side. All doubts had fled. There is something exciting about the resurrection. The darkness of the tomb could not contain the light of the world.

This same apostle was there when the tongues of fire (more lights) appeared in the upper room. When the surrounding people began to express their doubts—"They are full of new wine" (Acts 2:13b)—it was time to preach, and Peter was the one to do it. Operating in the revelation and power of this new Holy Spirit light, he called three thousand people to repentance in one day.

Considering these exciting happenings, I have a suggestion. Let's tell them—the people of this needy world—that we have a "great secret light." We do! Our light is the secret of creation, the secret of peace, the secret of life, of health, and of truth. And our Light is the remedy for darkness.

THE FIRST THING ON GOD'S AGENDA

We know light is the solution for darkness, don't we? Listen to God's first recorded words in the Bible. God's always had a voice. God could always speak. But the very first words we hear from God come to us from Genesis 1:1-3 (emphasis mine):

"In the beginning God created the heaven and the earth. And the earth was without form, and void; and *darkness* was upon the face of the deep. And the Spirit of God moved upon the face of the waters. And *God said, Let there be light: and there was light.*"

At that moment, the great contest had begun. Everything began with light versus darkness. God Almighty Himself was speaking, but to whom? I know! He was speaking to the darkness— this darkness that was over the whole earth. The cry of God came, "Let there be light!"

Instantly, the contest was over. Light had won. Darkness was defeated.

Before angels are introduced.

Before a place was defined that would demonstrate order.

Before people or even animals could exist, there had to be light.

Many have asked, "Which comes first—light or life?" The answer is easy. God Himself, who is light, supports all life. "This then is the message which we have heard of him, and declare unto you, that *God is light, and in him is no darkness at all*" (1 John 1:5, emphasis mine).

From the moment that God spoke the "light" word until right now, every time there has been a fight between light and darkness, light has won. Darkness has always been defeated. But there is still a problem. Jesus Himself gives the answer:

"Then spake Jesus again unto them, saying, *"I am the light of the world: he that followeth Me shall not walk in darkness, but shall have the light of life"* (John 8:12, emphasis mine).

"All things were made by Him, and without Him was not any thing made that was made. In him [this God-Light] was life, and the life was the light of men. *And the light shineth in darkness; and the darkness comprehended it not [could not grab it, perceive it or overcome it]"* (John 1:3-5, emphasis mine).

"I am come a light into world, that whoever believeth on me should not abide [live] in darkness (John 12:46, emphasis mine).

Now we understand: The world should come, must come to us! For every darkness, we have the light. Jesus said, and is still saying, "I am *the way, the truth, and the life*: no man cometh unto the Father, but by Me" (John 14:6, emphasis mine).

Not Mohammed, Buddha, Confucius—not anyone but Jesus.

CONTRAST OUR LIGHT WITH THE WORLD'S DARKNESS

To the darkness of religious confusion, our Light says, "I *am* the way."

To the darkness of all lies, our Light says, "I *am* the truth."

To the darkness of death that causes fear, our Light says, "I am the life."

To the darkness that brings torment of mind, our Light says, "Peace. Peace I leave with you, my peace I give unto you: not as the world giveth, give I unto you. Let not your heart be troubled, neither let it be afraid" (John 14:27).

THIS GOD-LIGHT, THROUGH JESUS, HAS COME TO PEOPLE LIKE US

"For God, *who commanded the light to shine out of darkness,* hath shined in our hearts, to give *the light* of the knowledge of the glory of God in *the face* [the revelation of His person and presence] of Jesus Christ" (2 Cor. 4:6, emphasis mine).

Saul of Tarsus is a fitting example. No one was more "messed-up" than he, but God turned him around and made a mighty apostle of him. When he stood before Agrippa, he was a powerful witness. He described what had happened to transform his life.

He did not say, "I came in contact with one of greater intelligence."

He did not say, "I met one more religious than I."

Nor did he say, "I met one with a more persuasive argument."

What he did say was this: "At midday, I saw in the way a light from heaven" (Acts 26:13b).

At that same appearance before King Agrippa, Paul revealed the purpose of his God-given message: to turn them from darkness to light (Acts 26:18b).

THE BROOKLYN TABERNACLE STORY

Jim Cymbala, pastor of the Brooklyn Tabernacle, came to our church in New Orleans. He told us of the transforming power of the Holy Spirit. He told us of the drug addicts and the prostitutes, pimps, and people on the brink of suicide who had found their way to the world-famous tabernacle in Brooklyn.

Then, for a joyful testimony in the flesh, he brought out individuals from their sixteen-member Brooklyn Tabernacle Chorus group. One by one, those who had once seemed hopeless stood by his side and told what the Light and Life—Jesus Christ—had done for them and in them. Pastor Cymbala had not come to merely speak of a Light that had once shined. He presented "lights" who were now standing before us singing, testifying, and shining to the brilliance of the Light.

GOD'S POWER OVER ALCOHOL

I have seen people come under the power of the gospel when they were drunk. I have prayed with many people "under the influence" and watched them come under a greater and more powerful influence: the power of God. I have watched them become instantly sober and healed in their bodies.

Many years ago, a man was brought to our church who had been in an automobile accident. Doctors had told him, "You will never be able to walk in a normal fashion." He half-stumbled and was half-carried down the aisle. He drank to ease the pain.

I did not realize it, but I asked him to do something he could not do: kneel. He was so crippled from his accident, there was no way he could kneel, but now the Word of God came —through my voice—telling him to kneel, and he did. We prayed, and he began to weep and to call on the name of the Lord, and in a matter of moments he was sober and standing up. He'd been miraculously saved and healed. He walked back to his seat without the crutches.

Afterward, this man was like the paint on the wall in our church. He was always there, for many, many months. He took every class we taught, and then one day, he walked into my office and said, "I'm going out to preach." He did. He preached his way around the world and is now pastoring a great church. What happened? He saw the light! In fact, he saw the Light of the World.

CHAPTER 23

Divine Direction (Real and Imagined)

O UR PROBLEMS OFTEN COME when we push against doors we want to open, but they are not God's open doors for us. I believe in hearing from God. I believe in prophecy, and I believe there are times when prophetic words of direction come to us, and these words reveal the possibilities of open doors and direction in our lives. The important thing to understand is that there must be a confirmation in one's own spirit, in one's own heart.

Something happened to me when I was nineteen years old that has become an example of how this should *not* happen. I was in my army barracks in Camp Barkley, Texas, sitting on my cot. It was my last night in this camp.

The next day, we would be leaving by train, going to St. Louis for some final administrative training before shipping out to India. Everybody in my group was speculating about our future—where we were ultimately going and what would happen to us.

I really wanted to hear a word of direction for my life. So I came up with an idea, one I had heard many other church people talk about. I decided to sit down with the Bible in my hands, close my eyes, and then open the Bible. With my eyes still closed, I'd place my finger somewhere on one of the pages. I'd then open my eyes, read the verses that were under my finger, and that would be the Word of God for me.

Everything was ready. My eyes were closed; I opened the Bible and placed my finger on one of the pages. I opened my eyes and began to read these words from Job 10:20-21, "Are not my days few? Cease then, and let me alone, that I may take comfort a little, Before I go whence I shall not return, even to the land of darkness and the shadow of death."

For a moment, fear gripped my heart, and then I closed the Bible and began to laugh at my foolish conduct. I knew God was not the author of fear and torment, and I knew this was not the way I would hear a word for my life.

A few weeks later, I was in a church in St. Louis. It was Sunday morning, and we were singing a beautiful worship song. A great peace touched my emotions, and I heard a strong inner voice telling me, "Fear not, for I will watch over you and bring you again to those you love. Trust me, for I have plans for you."

After I submitted my life to God for His plan for my life, one of my fears about the ministry was that I would have no place to go; no one would want me. This was another satanic and tormenting lie. The fact was, and my testimony to God's faithfulness is—that from the day I walked out of the university, there has never been one week when I did not have open doors and invitations to teach and preach the gospel. I did not have to make one telephone call or write one letter.

FOOLISH LEADERSHIP BY THE "PRECIOUS PROMISES"

When I was growing up, many people in our church and other churches had a little box, usually sitting on the kitchen table. Written on the box were these words: PRECIOUS PROMISES. About a hundred small cards were in the box, and on each card, there was a verse from the Bible containing some wonderful promise from the Word of God. The idea behind these was good.

The problems began when people started to use these little cards like fortunetellers use tea leaves and tarot cards. Some so-called fortunetellers use a deck of cards, and each card has a special message for people wanting to learn about their future, especially the future dealing with love, jobs, marriage, and money.

In the beginning of our ministry in New Orleans, the church was so small that I could always tell if someone were missing from the service. One new lady began to come to our church, but her attendance was rather erratic. She would be there one Sunday and then miss two Sundays before returning.

As I was standing at the door one Sunday morning, greeting the people as they left the service, she passed by, and I spoke to her. "We miss you when you are not here. Is there a problem Barbara and I can help you with?"

She smiled sweetly and said, "No, there is no problem, but I can only come to your church when God leads me to come."

My curiosity was in full operation, and I asked her, "How do you get direction from God when you are to attend our church?"

"I have a little box of 'Precious Promises.' Every Sunday morning, I sit at the table and pull out three cards and lay them facedown on the table. One card represents the Assembly of God church; another, the Church of God; and the final one represents your church. Whichever card has the most powerful verse, the greatest promise—that's where I go to church that morning. Sometimes, your card just does not come up."

She only showed up a few more times, and it was soon obvious that she had taken "my card" out of the box. This is foolish guidance at best, but more often, dangerous.

I once told this story in a public meeting, and one person came rebuking me, "Don't you know this is the way the apostles picked Judas' replacement? They cast lots to pick Matthias."

We really don't know what the apostles did. Perhaps they "drew straws." Perhaps they took two coins, drew a line in the sand, and then pitched the coins toward the line. The one that landed closest to the line would indicate which man would join them in the apostolic circle.

THE HOLY SPIRIT'S DIRECTION

There is one thing we do know. The Holy Spirit had not yet been poured out upon the apostles. God was with them, but He had not yet come to live in them. Once they were baptized in the Holy Spirit on the day of Pentecost, He became their guide; He gave them direction. Jesus told the disciples how they would receive understanding and revelation from God: "When he, the Spirit of truth [the Holy Spirit], is come, He will guide you into all truth: for He shall not speak of himself, but whatsoever he shall hear, that shall he speak; and he will shew you things to come" (John 16:13).

The church at Antioch knew when it was time to send out Barnabas and Saul as missionaries to the world. This report from Acts 13:2-3 tells the story: "As they ministered to the Lord, and fasted, the Holy Ghost said, 'Separate me Barnabas and Saul for the work whereunto I have called them.' And when they had fasted and prayed, and laid hands on them, they sent them away."

A genuine relationship with Jesus, the indwelling of His Holy Spirit, and a deep knowledge of the living Word of God will help us when we need guidance. We won't need to trust

in fingers pointed at Bible verses or cards drawn from a box
but in our loving, living walk with our Savior.

CHAPTER 24

Secrets of Survival; Examples of Victory

WHEN I WAS ABOUT thirteen years old, I made a shoeshine kit, went down to the main streets of Laurel, Mississippi, on Saturday morning, and shined shoes. If I had written a book on the subject, I would have called it *Seven Rules for Shining Shoes*. The rules would have been:

1. Make sure the shoes are clean.
2. Get good polish.
3. Spread it on evenly.
4. Let it dry.
5. Buff the shoes with a good, non-abrasive brush.
6. Put a little water on the shoes (that's where the term *spit shine* came into our vocabulary).
7. Finish with a good "shine" cloth.

My parents were afraid to give me the money for my weekly movie excursion, so I went down and shined shoes until I got enough for the movie, a hamburger, a candy bar, a Coke, and some popcorn. Then I would stash the shine box with one of my merchant friends and take off for the double-feature cowboy show. Wow!

HOW DID YOU SURVIVE?

As a successful New Orleans pastor, I was often invited to preach in different places. One afternoon, I was flying into the Memphis, Tennessee, airport. I casually looked out the window as we began to set down. I was thinking of the conference I would be attending, and I silently spoke to God. "Lord, help me to help these ministers."

I often pray this prayer. I never ask God to "Bless me," but I ask Him to "Bless Your people and let Your name be exalted." As I finished my short prayer, the Lord spoke to me with a strange question: "How did you survive?"

Immediately, I began to remember my struggles, my difficult times as a child and as a teenager, and in my early years of ministry. I especially remembered the condemnation of my church days. Our religious system knew a lot about law, but only a little about grace and mercy. Perhaps they had mental knowledge about these things, but we did not see it lived out in everyday experiences.

As I mentioned before, I grew up around much condemnation, and I watched many people go away. We drove them from the church. We were not only against evil, but we were against people. We must be against evil without destroying people. I hate evil, but I do not hate evil people. They are my harvest field.

When I went to Westerns as a young teen, people told me that if Jesus came, I would not "go up" if I were watching the Western movies. I did not believe that then, and I do not believe it now. I knew the grace and love of God and God's salvation were bigger than a movie. The day after I watched movies like this, I would go to church and sing the songs, pray the prayers and say "Amen" to the sermon. Sometimes the pastor would look down over the pulpit and tell the congregation, "We need more young people like Charles in our church."

As I was writing these words, I began to laugh. The cowboys and Jesus did a good job on me. I never turned away from God. But most of the young people in our church were gone before they were twenty-one. Many of them had been "condemned" out of the church. So, I guess watching Westerns was one way I survived!

When God asked me this question, I also remembered how we should answer God's questions. Ezekiel was smart when God questioned him. God caused him to see a valley of dry bones (a type of backslidden Israel). Then came the question. "Can these bones live?" Ezekiel's brilliant answer: "God, You know!" And so He did. Before this episode was finished, Ezekiel was prophesying to the dry bones, God was blowing the breath of His Spirit upon them, and they lived.

Now, when God said, "How did you survive?" I answered, "God, You know—tell me." And He did. I grabbed a pad and began to write. I hope that what I wrote in a few minutes on the plane helps and encourages you.

THINK IT—SAY IT—BELIEVE IT

If you are in the middle of a dirty and fearful nightmare, think first of survival. However, it isn't just about survival. You have to believe and confess, "I am not going to fail. I'm going to win!" You must trust and acknowledge that victory is coming. That being said, I have some suggestions on the following subjects: how to walk with God, how to come to maturity, how to fulfill your dreams, and how to experience victory. The only way that defeat is possible is if we are striving toward goals that are not God's.

I must confess, I don't like the word "survival" in and of itself. In anything I am doing for God, facing any problem that might arise, I never want to merely "survive." One man once sang me these words in a little song: "I don't mind the people staring; I don't mind the clothes I'm wearing; I don't mind my burdens bearing... if I can just make it in." To me, this sounds like weary desperation expressed to a God who cannot be trusted.

For me, while I survive, I want to travel on the road while rejoicing and becoming greatly victorious! Here is my list of six rules for survival and a victorious lifestyle. I have developed many of them through the practical but inspired experience I have developed in my walk with God. I will list these things, but I will not deal with them in detail. Details will come in my next book.

Here are the things God spoke to me.

1. We must believe God is a good God. Through the years, I have heard many people say, "God is a good God!" But I never learned to say it with conviction and power until I met Oral Roberts. I knew Oral for over thirty years, but I never became weary of hearing him say it. Until this day, when I hear him speak on a recording or see his face on a television screen, I want to cry out to him, "Say it, Oral. Say 'God is a good God!'" And almost every time--he does. Oral is now absent from the body and present with the Lord. He knows even more, on a deeply personal level, that God is a good God.

2. We must be able to perceive the grace of God.

"For ye know the grace of our Lord Jesus Christ, that, though he was rich, yet for your sakes he became poor, that ye through his poverty might be rich" (2 Cor. 8:9). The important thing is this: We must not only be able to perceive the grace of God; we must also have the revelation to receive it. Many Christians know the theology of God's grace, but they don't have the faith that they can partake of it. Sometimes that is a lack of revelation; at other times, it is self-condemnation—"I don't deserve it." My attitude today is that if God did not think I should have His grace, Jesus would not have died to bring me forgiveness and salvation.

3. We must learn that we can be renewed. Paul the apostle wrote to the church at Ephesus that they should not walk (lifestyle) as the Gentiles (heathen) walked, in the "futility of their mind." Then in Ephesians 4:22-23, he said these words: "Put off concerning the former conversation the old man. . . and be renewed in the spirit of your mind." The mind is the major source and arena of our battles; so if we want to do spiritual warfare, let's start with our minds.

4. We must trust in the rewards of a righteous lifestyle. Joseph never moved away from his righteous walk with God. He could have blamed God, his brothers, or the jailers for his many problems, but he did not. Know this—we are not talking about our personal good works. We must believe for the gracious acts of a loving God.

5. We must refuse to walk or live in condemnation. It is not what we have done or failed to do, but what Jesus did for us. I felt condemnation because I demanded perfection of myself. I was going to rescue the image of the ministry. That is a terrible load for anyone to bear.

What Jesus did for us makes us worthy because He is worthy. The foundation of the word "worthy" means we are "worth it." If God had not believed we were worth it, there would have been no blood, no cross.

One of my favorite verses is John 3:17: "For God sent not his Son into the world to condemn the world; but that the world through him might be saved." I also love:

There is therefore now no condemnation to them which are in Christ Jesus, [This is our position—we are "in Christ"] who walk not after the flesh, but after the Spirit. For the law of the Spirit of life in Christ Jesus hath made me free from the law of sin and death. For what the law could not do, in that it was weak through the flesh, God sending his own Son in the likeness of sinful flesh, and for sin, condemned sin in the flesh: That the righteousness of the law might be fulfilled in us, who walk not after the flesh, but after the Spirit (Rom. 8:1-4, emphasis mine).

6. WE MUST LEARN TO FORGIVE AND EVEN FORGET.

This principle is simple. It is a choice. Do we want hurt, bitterness, resentment, and even hatred to destroy us, or do we want God's blessings and His victory in our lives? Everyone experiences hurt and disappointments. These things can rule us, defile us, and destroy us—or we can learn to let them go, as Joseph did. We usually think about the Joseph story as it is presented in the book of Genesis, but in Psalm 105, we find some important additions.

We don't know all the feelings of Joseph during his trials—with his brothers, in Potiphar's house, and in prison. But there are some things we do know. He never walked away from God, and he never seemed to defy any authority. And what do we hear about him? The outstanding statement we hear many times is that "the Lord was with Joseph" (Gen. 39:2, 21). The following words of Paul are beautiful: "What shall we then say to these things? If God be for us, who can be against us? (Rom. 8:31) With Joseph, it did not seem to make any difference who or what was against him, because God was always for Him.

When Joseph became the second ruler in Egypt, you would think that, in the natural, it was payback time. I have often wondered about the time after all his struggles when he would have been riding the royal chariot down the road with all Pharaoh's people around him. Where was Potiphar's wife—the wife who had lied about him and had him put in prison? If she were in the crowd, I wonder what she was thinking?

We do know Pharaoh gave Joseph the daughter of a heathen priest to be his wife. We never see that she had any influence over Joseph. It is evident that He brought her to the knowledge of the true God. The Bible tells us, during the seven years of plenty, that Joseph had two sons: And Joseph called the name of the firstborn Manasseh: "For *God, said he, has made me forget* all my toil, and all my father's house." And the name of the second was Ephraim: "For God hath caused me to be fruitful in the land of my affliction" (Gen 41:51-52, emphasis mine).

Notice that we see no hatred, bitterness, or revenge. And notice that the name of the first son meant "forgiveness," while the name of the second son meant "fruitfulness." How wonderful that God gave Joseph the spirit of forgetting before fruitfulness came along. If the fruitfulness had come first, he could have brought forth bitterness. When I come to the end of my journey, I do not want to present bitter fruit as an offering to God. I think Joseph's statement in verse 52 is so wonderful: "God hath caused me to be fruitful in the land of my affliction." This is much different from the natural human response.

Also when Joseph's brothers finally came to Egypt for food, he played games with them for a time, but you see his real spirit when he is weeping and rejoicing with them as their relationship is restored. I also have no bitterness toward the ice cream company that paid me only ten cents an hour. If I could find it again, I would thank my bosses for giving me a job and teaching me a work ethic that has lasted all through my life. God has also caused me to be fruitful as He's brought me through the land of my affliction.

MY GREAT HEROES

When I was nine years old, my parents bought me a copy of Egermeier's *Bible Story Book*. When my mother died on December 7, 1994, at the age of eighty-eight, I found my old book among her treasures. The leaves were worn, the binding about gone, and I sent it to a bookbinder who was recommended to me. It is now in excellent condition again. I thank God for Elsie Egermeier who wrote the stories in my book. These Bible stories were some of the important factors affecting my life.

I had many heroes when I was growing up. I liked Superman, Batman, and Captain Marvel. Even today, when I get excited about something, I say, "Shazam!"—the word Captain Marvel said that brought an instant power transformation. However, because of Elsie Egermeier's book, my biggest heroes have always been in the Bible.

CHAPTER 25

No Condemnation

AFTER MY MIRACLE NIGHT, I learned to move away from harsh opinions. Sometimes the Holy Spirit would whisper to me, "Slow down; don't be so pushy. Don't ram your will and opinions down everybody's throats. Be gentler and give others time to catch up to your vision."

I learned in my struggle and after my deliverance that renewal starts in the mind. We have a choice. We can have a futile mind—untrustworthy, worthless—or we can have a renewed mind. It looks so easy as I sit here and write these words, but when I go through hellish battles, I often forget to apply the most elementary rules of a godly life.

"CONFESS WITH THY MOUTH"

Through all my torment, I never developed a negative attitude toward God. I walked and drove through the city, constantly confessing that God loved me and was going to deliver me. When I was alone, I spoke the confession with my mouth.

My life and ministry were built on Romans 10:9, "That if thou shalt confess with thy mouth the Lord Jesus, and shalt believe in thine heart that God hath raised him from the dead, thou shalt be saved [total salvation, healing and deliverance from every bondage, from the Greek word *sozo*]." I believed the Word. I confessed the Word. And the Word worked mightily in me—and it will work in you.

This is the way it was with Joseph. God *was* with him. One day he was a prisoner—a nobody. The next day he was the prime minister of Egypt, second in command to Pharaoh. Archie Dennis, one of my dear friends, who has gone home to be with the Lord, attested to this. While he was living, he wrote a powerful song, "I've Never Seen the Righteous Forsaken." In it, Archie wrote:

You may be down today, but help is on the way.
Dark clouds may dim the skies, but He'll answer you by
   and by,
Because I've never seen the righteous forsaken
Nor His seed out begging for bread.

David writes about this testimony in Psalm 37:23-25 (emphasis mine): "The steps of a good man are ordered by the Lord: and he delighteth in his way. Though he fall, he shall not be utterly cast down: for the Lord upholdeth him with his hand. I have been young, and now am old; *yet I have not seen the righteous forsaken, nor his seed [descendants] be begging bread."*

Consider Job. People hear a lot about the troubles and problems of Job. But Job survived and came forth to a much greater victory because he had a strong testimony about God.

All the while as my breath is in me, and the spirit of God is in my nostrils; my lips shall not speak wickedness, nor my tongue utter deceit. God forbid that I should justify you: till I die I will not remove mine integrity from me. My righteousness I hold fast, and will not let it go: my heart shall not reproach me so long as I live (Job 27:3-6).

When we move into the New Testament, the positive and victorious testimonies keep coming. Here is a great one from Paul, the apostle:

> *[It is] not by works of righteousness which we have done, but according to His mercy He saved us, by the washing of regeneration, and renewing of the Holy Ghost, which He shed on us abundantly through Jesus Christ our Savior; that being justified by his grace, we should be made heirs according to the hope of eternal life (Titus 3:5-7).*

If we confess the greatness of God, we come through our trials with a higher, more joyful perspective. That only happens through God working and renewing one's mind.

ORAL ROBERTS' FAITH PROBLEM

At one time or another, everyone has experienced a faith problem. There is no shame in that. Can you imagine Oral Roberts with a crisis of faith? Oral looked me in the face and told me about his problem--not once but many times.

Your mind must be running a thousand miles an hour. What was Oral Roberts' area of unbelief? It was simple. I often asked him to tell me about the success of his tent revivals. He would invariably say, "I could have faith for miracles, but I did not have faith for crowds."

He told me how he would arrange the seats in the big revival tent. Because he was afraid nobody would come, he would leave a lot of space on the right and left side of every seat, and he would start the rows from front to back with at least five to six feet between them. In the beginning, it made the tent look full when it was only half-full.

As God began to move and miracles began to happen, the crowds grew. Every night, Oral would have his workers move the chairs just a little closer together, until finally, the people would have to squeeze to get into their seats. However, no matter how big the crowd was at the end of a series of meetings, when the next meeting started, he did not have faith to believe that people would show up. And there was plenty of room between and around those chairs once more.

REFUSE TO WALK OR LIVE IN CONDEMNATION

One basic premise we should never forget is this: Jesus did not come to condemn us. Therefore, we should not let anyone else condemn us, nor should we go around condemning ourselves. We are all familiar with John 3:16, but we should also pay close attention to the words of John 3:17. "For God sent not His Son into the world to condemn the world; but that the world through Him might be saved."

However, if we rebel against God by rejecting Him and His Word, we automatically come under condemnation. So the choice is ours. Receive Him and get life and salvation. Reject Him and get death and condemnation. God's Word states these facts very clearly:

"He that believeth on him is not condemned: *but he that believeth not is condemned already, because he hath not believed in the name of the only begotten Son of God. And this is the condemnation,* that light is come into the world, and men loved darkness rather than the light, because their deeds were evil (John 3:18-19, emphasis mine).

During times of temptation, God will help us if we will let Him.

"Therefore hath no temptation taken you *but such as is common to man: but God is faithful,* who will not suffer you to be tempted above that ye are able, but will with the temptation *also make a way to escape,* that ye may be able to bear it" (1 Cor. 10:13, emphasis mine).

Blessed is the man that endureth temptation: for when he is tried, he shall receive the crown of life, which the Lord hath promised to them that love him. Let no man say when he is tempted, I am tempted of God: for God cannot be tempted with evil, neither tempteth he any man: But every man is tempted, when he is drawn away by his own lust, and enticed. Then when lust hath conceived, it bringeth forth sin: and sin, when it is finished, bringeth forth death (James 1:12-15).

The development of sin is like this. Lust draws us in the wrong direction, but we don't have to follow that path. We don't have to give birth to sin. As we anticipate it, and when it starts, sin often seems pleasant, but when it is finished, it brings forth death. The "rush" of drugs in the beginning seems pleasurable, but when our brains are fried, we experience the horror of total dependence on an ungodly evil.

Joseph learned to trust God and forgive—and so can we. Let me state it again: It did not seem to make any difference to Joseph who was against him, because God was always for Him. I love the words of this song we used to sing, written by Stuart Hamblen. These words also kept me company during the difficult nights.

If God be for us, who can stand against us?
He's that Rock in a weary land,
He has worlds at His command,
We cannot fall with His mighty arms around us;
His Word is stronger than the mighty sword.

PAUL'S AFFLICTIONS DID NOT PRODUCE BITTERNESS

Paul could have hated the Jewish people for what they did to him, but we find his true feelings in Romans 10:1: "My heart's desire and prayer to God for Israel is that they might be saved."

Brethren, I count not myself to have apprehended: but *this one thing I do, forgetting those things which are behind, and reaching forth* unto those things which are before, I press toward the mark for the *prize of the high calling of God in Christ Jesus* (Phil. 3:13, emphasis mine).

"Forgetting," "reaching," "I press," "the high calling of God in Christ Jesus. It doesn't get any better than this!

CHAPTER 26

Living in Marvelous Light

ALL THESE WORDS I have written—they are true. These things really happened to me, and as I close, I want to share with you the way I live now—the confessions I still make as I walk with God.

I not only have faith for healing, but I walk in faith for my constant wellness. At this time, I have not had a common cold in the last eleven years. During the past thirteen years, I have spent only three days in the "sick bed."

There are reasons for this. My lifestyle is partly responsible. I have never smoked, drunk alcohol, or lived an unclean lifestyle. To keep my weight down, I have exercised regularly through the years. I have run thousands of miles around tracks and through the streets of New Orleans from the time

I was thirty-five years old until I was seventy. At that time, I changed the running to a fast walk.

All of this is good, but it is not the whole story. The most important thing is my walk with God. I love God; I often confess this love directly to Him. And this is my revelation confession—I live under the divine favor of God. My heavenly Father watches over me! I haven't earned this relationship, but I still live under the grace, mercy, and favor of God. This is my testimony. It can become your testimony as well.

MY POSITIVE CONFESSIONS

When I go through any kind of pressure or problem, I don't give in to it. Instead, I start my positive confessions. I recommend that you confess them too.

1. I am going to walk out of darkness and bathe in the light of the glory of God.

2. I am going to believe for my healing and complete deliverance from every power of hell that tries to destroy me.

3. I am ready once again to make a total commitment to God, His Word, and His Kingdom.

4. I know and will believe that God is a good God. He loves me!

5. I will trust in His grace and believe He extends it to me.

6. I will not give up. I insist on being renewed.

7. I believe there is a godly reward for a righteous lifestyle.

8. I will not only forgive the past, but I will not dwell on it. I will put it out of my mind.

THE OVERCOMING POWER OF GOD

Let me urge you: never surrender to the devil or believe his words. When Jesus was speaking to the Pharisees of religion, He gave this warning:

Ye are of your father the devil, and the lusts of your father ye will do. He was a murderer from the beginning, and abode not in the truth, because *there is no truth in him.* When he speaketh a lie, he speaketh of his own: for *he is a liar, and the father of it* (John 8:44, emphasis mine).

These words are of utmost importance! There is no truth in the devil. He is a liar and the father of lies. When he talks to us, we should believe the exact opposite of what he says.

God, on the other hand, "giveth more grace. Wherefore he saith, God resisteth the proud, but giveth grace unto the humble. *Submit yourselves therefore to God. Resist the devil, and he will flee from you.* Draw nigh to God, and he will draw nigh to you. Cleanse your hands, ye sinners; and purify your hearts, ye double minded (James 4:6-8 emphasis mine).

Notice the progression here. First, we submit to God. This is not merely believing in God. *This is the turning of our lives, our desires, our plans, and our futures over to God.* I have heard people say, "I have made Jesus my Savior, but I have not yet made Him my Lord." When we deny his lordship, we are certainly not children of God. Joining the family means submitting to the Chief Executive Officer and to apostolic authority.

The second part commands that we resist the devil. With him, deceit is the norm, hate is the norm, confusion is the norm. All things negative and destructive are the norm. So what do we do? We must resist and do the exact opposite of what the devil says to us. When he whispers, "You are going to fail," that means you are going to succeed in God's plan. When he says, "You are going to die," you are going to live. If we have submitted to God, we do not have to submit to the devil. We can resist him, and he will flee!

In the Bible, there is no true faith apart from obedience to the Word of God. If we truly believe, the marks of that obedience will be submission to God's Word, His will, and His way.

Margaret E. Barber, born in 1869, communicates my sentiments exactly in this old song. Don't be intimidated by her archaic phrasing. Read it aloud.

I dare not be defeated with Calvary in view,
Where Jesus conquered Satan, where all His foes
   He slew;
Come, Lord, give me a vision, prepare me for the fight.
Make me an overcomer, clothed with the Spirit's might.
I dare not be defeated since Christ, my conquering King
Has called me to the battle, which He did surely win.
Come, Lord, give me courage to battle for the right;
Make me an overcomer, clothed with the Spirit's might.

I dare not be defeated when Jesus leads me on,
To press through hellish legions, to share with him
the throne.
Come, Lord, and give thy soldier the power to wield
the sword;
Make me an overcomer, through Thine inerrant Word.
I dare not be defeated, just at the set of the sun,
When Jesus waits to whisper, "Well done, beloved,
well done."
Lord, clothe me with Thy Spirit;
Thy power to me now send.
Make me an overcomer, a victor to the end!

—"I Dare Not Be Defeated,"
Margaret E. Barber, public domain

Endorsements

I have known Charles Green since 1965, just after a hunting accident in which Gloria's 14-year-old brother Richard almost lost his hand. We took him to New Orleans for surgery, where I was supernaturally led to the name of the church Charles pastored.

I called the church phone number listed in the phone book, and Charles answered the phone that he hardly ever answered. I told him about the situation, and he came to Richard's hospital room, prayed over him, and prophesied that he would be better in basketball the next season. That was in November, and Richard went from almost losing his hand to, just as Charles prophesied, lettering in basketball.

Light of Victory is a book every Christian should read—now! It should especially be read by everyone in the ministry of the Lord Jesus. Charles is ninety-three years old and still traveling the world preaching victory.

JESUS IS LORD!

—Kenneth Copeland, Fort Worth, Texas

Fear is a topic we all deal with every day in one way or another. We often don't understand how it affects our lives in a negative way through its ability to cause us to become powerless and ineffective.

Charles Green's personal journey sheds light on the topic and allows us to put his conclusions into action in our own lives. His book enables us to overcome our fears through powerful insights from the Word of God. It empowers us to recognize how to deal with fear and realize the power of the Holy Spirit in this process. The Word of God can lead us out of fear and into power through the words which we read and implement.

I'm so grateful Dr. Green has shared a pathway to overcome fear and live in victory. It is a powerful teaching for this time in our lives when so many people suffer needlessly from fear.

—Dr. Glenda Pavas, DMD

Tulsa, Oklahoma

Wow! Are you ready for an encounter with God? Dr. Green has opened a dark time in his life that very few people, especially ministers, would dare share so openly for fear of rejection and condemnation.

This book is for anyone who is living with a dark cloud over their life or struggling to get free from the prison of their mind that is forged by the master tormentor, Satan. This book will change your life!

Thank you, Dr. Green, for being so transparent with your personal life story so that many captives can be set free. I immediately thought of several family members and friends who need this word, and I'll make sure to give them each a copy of your book. This is a book that must be in every church bookstore and library.

—Bishop Bart Pierce
Rock City Church of Baltimore, Maryland

My life has been a wonderful experience of following God's call, a call activated and confirmed at Word of Faith in the early sixties.

Whenever I am asked about what influence had the most effect on my life, I respond that I learned more about ministry and how to conduct myself from Charles Green than any other teacher, trainer, or mentor I ever had. Your confidence in me and the opportunities you provided for me to minister have had lifelong positive effects. I urge everyone to read this book!

—Bishop Gordon McDonald,
General Superintendent, Pentecostal Holiness Church
of Canada